THE

THRILL

OF THE

CHASTE

"Writing from her personal experience, Dawn Eden illuminates a path through our devastated hookup culture using practical wisdom and theological insight from a woman's perspective."

Rev. Mark Mary
Cohost of EWTN's *Life on the Rock*

"Dawn Eden's wry, poignant *Thrill of the Chaste* isn't just another chastity primer but the narrative of a soul redemptively recovering from Gen-X cynicism. Her raw chronicles conjure awkwardly familiar memories without glamorizing sin, all the while focusing on changing the person, not the past, and doing so with the hope of Christ."

Colleen Swaim
Author of *Your College Faith*

"According to Jesus Christ—and Dawn Eden—chastity is part of the Good News. Only a pure heart can be a fulfilled heart. Dawn Eden has given us a practical and joyful guide to chaste living."

Rev. Paul N. Check
Executive Director
Courage International

"Dawn Eden's book helped me to understand that virtue is about much more than our sexuality; its pursuit is a positive action applicable to our work, our relationships, our prayer, our play, our daily bread—indeed, it is applicable to every aspect of our lives. So is this book."

Elizabeth Scalia
Catholic blogger and author of *Strange Gods*

"Very few writers can crank out prose that is at once elegant and funny, engaging and eclectic, and spiritually enriching with no treacly aftereffects—a combination that sums up Dawn Eden's sweet spot as a new evangelist. I know her sorrow-tinged but ever hopeful story is going to change lives."

Patrick Coffin
Author and host of *Catholic Answers Live*

♡ Dawn Eden

DAWN EDEN

CATHOLIC
EDITION

THE

THRILL

OF THE

CHASTE

FINDING FULFILLMENT
WHILE KEEPING YOUR CLOTHES ON

AVE MARIA PRESS AVE Notre Dame, Indiana

Founded in 1865, Ave Maria Press is a ministry of the United States Province of Holy Cross.

www.avemariapress.com

Paperback: ISBN-13 978-1-59471-558-7

E-book: ISBN-13 978-1-59471-559-4

Cover image © Undrey/Dollar Photo Club

Text design by Katherine Robinson.

Printed and bound in the United States of America.

Library of Congress Cataloging-in-Publication Data

Eden, Dawn, 1968-

The thrill of the chaste : finding fulfillment while keeping your clothes on / Dawn Eden. -- Catholic Edition.

pages cm

Includes bibliographical references.

ISBN 978-1-59471-558-7 -- ISBN 1-59471-558-0

1. Single women--Religious life. 2. Single women--Conduct of life. 3. Single women--Sexual behavior. 4. Christian women--Conduct of life. 5. Chastity. 6. Sexual abstinence--Religious aspects--Christianity. I. Title.

BV4596.S5E34 2015

241'.664--dc23

2014037316

To Father Francis Canavan, S.J. (1917–2009),

who taught me that "we cannot begin if we insist on

beginning with certainty,"

and whose spiritual fatherhood showed me how to

live my *Suscipe* as he lived his own,

seeking the God who is "absolute Being, absolute

Good, and absolute Beauty,"

this book is lovingly dedicated.

CONTENTS

Foreword by Colleen Carroll Campbell~**ix**

Preface to the Catholic Edition~**xiii**

Chapter 1
Not the Same Old Song~**1**

Chapter 2
Why It's Easy to Blame Mom and Dad
(and Why You Shouldn't)~**13**

Chapter 3
My Journey Home (to Rome)~**21**

Chapter 4
The First Cut Is the Deepest~**31**

Chapter 5
The Meaning of Sex~**43**

Chapter 6
Gaining Self-Control Without Losing Your Mind~**53**

Chapter 7
Becoming a Singular Sensation~**63**

Chapter 8
The Agony and the Ecstasy~**73**

Chapter 9
Saying Yes Like You Mean It~**81**

Chapter 10
Tender Mercies: Reconnecting with Your Vulnerability~**91**

Chapter 11
The Iniquity of My Heels~101

Chapter 12
How Beginnings Shape Endings~111

Chapter 13
Answering the Call~119

Chapter 14
The Gift of the Present Moment~123

Chapter 15
Living Modestly~133

Chapter 16
A Thorny Issue: Dealing with Temptation~141

Chapter 17
Winning the Spiritual Battle~151

Chapter 18
Why Shared Values Matter~161

Chapter 19
Believing Is Seeing~173

Chapter 20
Craving Heaven~185

Notes~197

FOREWORD

I first heard of Dawn Eden's *The Thrill of the Chaste* shortly after its 2006 publication. Several of her fans wrote urging me to read the book and interview her on my television show *Faith & Culture*. I did both and was glad I did.

In a sea of Christian chastity primers penned mostly for teens and college students and too often characterized by a cloying sentimentalism that trivializes the challenges and rewards of living chastely, Dawn's book stood out. She spoke to the walking wounded of the sexual revolution, the men and women who already had wasted years wandering down the dead-end path of our hook-up culture. They needed a frank, compassionate guide to an exit strategy. Many of them found it in the witty, wise pages of *The Thrill of the Chaste*.

It was a good book.

This one is better.

I do not say that only because this new version draws on the depth and insights of the saints, Church Fathers, and Catholic teaching in a way that the original did not. Those elements undoubtedly enrich this new work, as do the years that Dawn has spent living and studying her Catholic faith since writing the original.

Nor do I say that simply because this new version retains the best of the old: namely, its humor and brutal honesty. I know from firsthand experience that the hardest part of writing a spiritual memoir is telling your story as it actually happened, not as you wish it had happened. It's scary to admit in print your faults and false starts, your repeated stumbles, and the very vulnerabilities you've spent decades trying to conceal.

Thankfully for her readers, Dawn overcame that fear. In this new version, she reveals some of her most painful and humiliating memories—including the sexual abuse she suffered as a child, which left an ache she later tried to numb with casual sex. Dawn shares these recollections without sensationalism or self-pity in an effort to point readers beyond her dark times and theirs toward the healing light of Christ.

Perhaps equally boldly, Dawn refuses to sugarcoat the challenges that come with embracing chastity in our porn-saturated, sex-obsessed culture. Skeptics considering a turn toward chastity will find credible, concrete help here. So will already chaste singles struggling to keep the faith while navigating a social scene that tests them at every turn. Even consecrated and married men and women who have been walking the road of chastity for years can benefit from Dawn's reflections on the less obvious obstacles to achieving greater freedom in Christ.

That's not the most important achievement of this new version, though. What sets it apart is its unflinching focus on the ultimate end of all our striving: the eternal, ecstatic vision of God that awaits the pure of heart.

"Blessed are the pure of heart," Jesus tells us, "for they shall see God" (Mt 5:8). Dawn takes this promise seriously. Throughout this new book, she reminds us that chastity's reward is not merely a well-ordered life or healthier relationships. Its final fruit is a transforming union with God, a union we can begin to experience on earth even as we await its final fulfillment in heaven.

That's important because, as Dawn discovered on her own journey, an empty space exists inside each of us, whether single, married, or consecrated, that can be filled only by God. Chastity allows us to recognize that truth. We see that our sexual desires exist not merely for their own sake—as our culture tells us—or only to help us make babies and strengthen marriages, as important as those two goods are. Our desires also exist to help us learn to love as God loves, and to point us toward the One who will someday quench our infinite thirst for love.

That's the secret joy of this once-revered, now-reviled virtue. Dawn knows it in her depths. Her willingness to share her hard-won wisdom in this brave book is itself proof of chastity's liberating, life-changing power.

Colleen Carroll Campbell
Author of *My Sisters the Saints: A Spiritual Memoir*

PREFACE TO THE
CATHOLIC EDITION

Chastity, like me, has long suffered from a
bad reputation—only in chastity's case, it's
undeserved.

Those words, opening the introduction to the first edition of
The Thrill of the Chaste, went farther than I ever could have
imagined when I wrote them in my apartment in Hoboken, New Jersey. Judging from the hundreds of responses
I have received from readers, they reached every continent
of the world except Antarctica. (I still hold out hope that
some joyfully chaste person down there will dip a penguin
feather in ink and drop me a line.)

The more memorable responses to *The Thrill* included
an invitation to the wedding of an Irish reader (she credited
the book for bringing her back to Catholic faith) and dozens
of fan letters from seminarians thanking me for encouraging them in their vocation. The seminarians' reaction
was what surprised me the most. Given that, at the time I
was writing the book, I was hoping for marriage, it wasn't
exactly the kind of male reaction I was looking for—but it
was deeply gratifying nonetheless.

When I wrote *The Thrill*, in late 2005, my life was much
different than it is today. Then, I was in my mid-thirties,
working full time on the editorial staff of the *New York
Daily News*. My spiritual journey to Rome was not yet

complete—I was a Jewish convert to Protestant Christianity, preparing via RCIA (Rite of Christian Initiation of Adults) to make the final leap into the Catholic Church—and I now know that my vocational journey was not complete either.

Today, I write and speak on healing from childhood sexual abuse—the message of my second book, *My Peace I Give You* (Ave Maria Press, 2012). In my personal life, I am working to complete a pontifical doctorate in theology (which, by some cruel joke on chaste people, is called an STD) and have done something I would not have imagined in 2005: I made a personal consecration of my celibacy to the Sacred Heart of Jesus through the Immaculate Heart of Mary.

The invitation from Ave Maria Press editor Kristi McDonald to do a new edition of *The Thrill* was like the answer to an unspoken prayer. I had long wished I could revise the work, for several reasons.

First, practically from the moment the book went to press, I regretted filling it with references to the television show *Sex and the City* and other pop-culture fads that very quickly became dated. Second, the response not only from seminarians but also from other male readers made me wish I had addressed the book to men and women, rather than just women. (The focus on women also opened me to accusations that I was promoting a double standard for chastity, which was certainly not my intention.) Third, as a Catholic (since 2006), I wanted to show readers how the richness of the sacramental life of the Church gives strength and inspiration to those seeking to live according to God's plan. Finally, I wanted to speak more directly to readers who suffer sexual wounds, drawing upon the spirituality of healing that I developed in *My Peace I Give You*.

I remain grateful to everyone I acknowledged in the first edition, including especially my family and my agent, Janet Rosen of the Sheree Bykofsky Agency, and also my former *New York Post* colleagues Col Allan and Susan

Edelman, without whom this book would not exist (see chapter 7 of *My Peace I Give You* and Gn 50:20). For this edition, I would like to also thank Kristi McDonald and everyone at Ave Maria Press, Wes Yoder and everyone at the Ambassador Agency, and Lyle Brooks.

NOT THE SAME OLD SONG

Late one night in the fall of 2004, walking home from the underground rail station after putting in a shift at my newspaper job, I passed by a restaurant as it was shutting down for the evening. Casting a sideways glance into the windows of the eatery—a burger joint meant to evoke the 1950s, when rock and roll was born—I could see the bored waiters in their starched white uniforms and matching caps as they wiped the chrome tabletops. One last tune crackled from the outdoor speakers onto the deserted streets: the Shirelles' "Will You Love Me Tomorrow."

To say I knew the song well would be an understatement, even though it was a hit years before I was born. I knew all the statistics about it, the way a sports fan knows all the statistics about the players on his favorite team. I knew who wrote the song (husband-and-wife team Gerry Goffin and Carole King), what company released it (Scepter), when it came out (1960), how high it got on the charts (number one), and how the Shirelles got their name (from

I

lead singer Shirley Owens). I knew that the Beatles admired
the song and had performed it onstage—with John Lennon
singing lead!—before they became a worldwide sensation.
All this I knew because, in a previous career, I had been a
rock historian, writing for music magazines about the stories behind old pop songs.

Hearing Shirley Owens's plaintive voice took me back
to those days when I sought fulfillment in the exhilarat-
ing highs of rock concerts; in attempts to win love through
giving my body; in cynical efforts to get pleasure from
men who I knew in my heart could not love me—really, in
almost anything except the love of Jesus Christ.

The words of "Will You Love Me Tomorrow," too,
brought up bittersweet memories—more bitter than sweet.
Like many songs from that more innocent era, the song
expresses feelings that most people would be too ashamed
to verbalize. There's something painful about the way its
vulnerable heroine leaves herself wide open. She's not looking for affirmation so much as absolution. All her man has
to do is say he loves her—then a night of sin is transformed
into a thing of beauty.

◆ ◆ ◆

We hear a lot today about "human rights," but did you ever
stop to think about what exactly is a right? Is a right simply
something that the government gives us? Or is it something
that people are due by virtue of being human?

As a young, unmarried woman before I knew the
"thrill of the chaste," I used to think of having an active
sex life as a basic human right. I had the right to vote, the
right to free speech, the right to freedom of religion (or,
in my case, freedom from religion), and the right to seek
sexual pleasure however I wished.

It's safe to say I wasn't alone in my sense of entitlement. Practically all the popular movies, television

programs, electronic media, books, magazines, and songs urge the unmarried to take the sexual pleasure that's due them. While love is celebrated, we are assured that a satisfying sexual encounter does not require love. If the Shirelles tune were written today, the singer would likely have to lower the bar down to "Will You Respect Me Tomorrow"—if even that.

The fruits of this accepted single-person lifestyle resemble those of a drug habit more than a dating paradigm. Unmarried men and women become caught in a vicious cycle. They feel lonely because they are not loved, so they lend their bodies to "lovers" who do not love them.

That was my life.

When I was twenty, my boyfriend left me for a friend of mine who—unlike me—had sexual experience. A rock musician (as was pretty much every man I liked back then), he had been a long-distance beau for two years, and I had dreamed of having him live nearby. When he finally moved to New York City, just across Central Park from my Upper West Side apartment, we celebrated together. But only a month later, he told me it was over between us, without giving a reason. More time passed before he could gather the courage to admit that my own friend—who had recently stopped calling me—had become his new love.

What I took from that rejection was that I had to gain sexual experience if I wanted to have any chance of keeping a man. In theory, the task would be laughably easy. I was living in the heart of New York City—not exactly a bastion of prudery—and was immersed in the freewheeling world of rock nightclubs.

Yet, although I saw nothing morally wrong with engaging in sexual activity outside of marriage, it was hard for me to convince myself that my virginity was not worth saving for someone special. However much I told myself it didn't matter, I wanted my first time to be with someone I could be sure really *would* love me tomorrow.

But I couldn't hold out forever. Not one of my friends from the rock world was still a virgin (or, if they were, they weren't admitting it). What's more, nothing I saw—be it movies, television shows, or my experience of New York City nightlife—suggested that love would wait for sex. If anything, it seemed to be the other way around. Both in fiction and in the real world, people seemed not so much to fall in love as to slide into sexual relationships that perhaps turned into love somewhere along the way.

I ended up losing my virginity at age twenty-three to a man I found attractive but didn't love—just to get it out of the way.

◆ ◆ ◆

Instead of becoming supremely self-confident in the wake of my newfound experience, I only became more insecure. It was soon clear that, while getting a man to take a sexual interest in me was easy, getting him to think of me as a serious girlfriend was not.

No matter how hard I tried, I couldn't transform a sexual encounter—or string of encounters—into a real relationship. The most I could hope for was a man who would treat me with "respect" but who really wouldn't have any concern for me once we split the tab for breakfast.

That's not to say I didn't meet any nice guys while I was casually dating. I did, but either they seemed boring—as nice guys so often do when you're used to players—or I inadvertently snuffed out the budding relationship by trying to rush things.

Don't get me wrong; I wasn't insatiable. I was insecure.

When you're insecure, you fear losing control. In my case, the main way I thought I could control a relationship was by either introducing a sexual component or allowing my boyfriend to do so.

Either way, I would end up alone and unhappy, but I didn't know how else to handle a relationship. I felt trapped in a lifestyle that gave me none of the things that the media and popular wisdom promised it would.

Some friends and family, trying to be helpful, would counsel me to simply stop looking. I did manage to stop looking, sometimes for months at a time. But then, when I would meet a potential boyfriend, I'd once again bring the relationship down to the lowest common denominator.

I hated the seeming inevitability of it all—how each of my attempts at a relationship would implode—yet, in some strange way, it seemed safe. By speeding things up sexually, I was saving myself from being rejected—or worse, ignored—if I moved too slowly. After all, if I was eventually going to be rejected anyway, I thought I should at least get something out of it—if only one night of enjoying the illusion of being wanted.

It all sounds terribly cynical as I reflect upon it now—and it was. I was lonely and depressed, and I had painted myself into a corner.

◆ ◆ ◆

In October 1999, at the age of thirty-one, my life changed radically when, after being an agnostic Jew for my entire adult life, I had a religious experience that convinced me of the truth of Christian faith. Having read the gospels, I had long believed that Jesus was a good man. What changed me was realizing for the first time that he was more than a man—he was truly God's Son. (A few years later, after trying to live the Christian life as a Protestant, my faith would undergo a new transformation as I learned that Jesus remains really present on earth through the Eucharist, but I'll save that story for chapter 3.)

With my newfound faith came a sudden awareness that I badly needed to "get with the program"—especially where my sex life was concerned. But even being aware of what had to be done, I had a long way to go between realizing what was wrong with my behavior and actually changing it.

Thankfully, over time, I found that whenever I was tempted to return to the vicious cycle (meet intriguing guy, offer my body, dump or be dumped, repeat), a new thought would emerge to give me pause—an antidote to the pleasure principle. I call it the tomorrow principle.

◆ ◆ ◆

I discovered the tomorrow principle at a time when, having made the decision to be chaste, I was struggling each day to overcome damaging habits—the fallback behaviors that might temporarily assuage my loneliness but ultimately left me feeling empty. Every day, it was a trial to resist contacting an ex-lover or scouring the Internet personals to find a new one. At night, when my loneliness hit hardest, I had to fight the temptation to put on my most revealing clothes (which I could not yet bear to throw out, even though they made me look like an epidermis buffet) and go to a party or nightclub where I could feel sexy—if not lovable.

Staying up through the wee hours one morning— during that fleeting window of time when everything is quiet, even the online social chatter—I typed out a reflection on where I was and where I wanted to be:

> All my adult life, I've struggled with my weight. When I'm walking home at the end of the day, there's nothing I want more than a bag of fried cheese-flavored snacks or malted-milk balls. If I'm trying to slim down—which is most of the time—it's hard, really hard, to think of why I can't have what I'm craving.
> The little devil on my left shoulder is saying, "Get the Cheez Doodles. You'll be satisfied, and

you won't gain weight. Even if you do gain, it'll be less than a pound—you can lose it the next day."

And you know what? He's right. If I look at it in a vacuum, one indiscretion is not going to do any damage that can't be undone.

Then the little angel on my right shoulder speaks up. "Uh-uh. If you buy those Cheez Doodles, you know what's going to happen."

"I'll get orange fingerprints on the pages of the novel I'm reading tonight?" I reply.

The angel lets that one go by. "You'll buy them again tomorrow night," he nags. "And the next night."

"Remember what happened during the fall of your freshman year of high school," the angel goes on, "when the student clubs held after-school bake sales every day? Remember how you discovered that if you waited around long enough, all the goodies would be discounted 'til you could get a lemon square and three chocolate-chip cookies for fifty cents?"

"Please—" I groan. I know where this is going. The devil on my left shoulder is pulling my hair in the direction of the snack-foods aisle.

"And remember," the angel continues, smelling victory, "how your jeans kept getting tighter and tighter? And you had to—"

"I know," I say, exasperatedly.

"You had to lie down to zip them up," he says triumphantly. "Finally, one by one, you busted the fly on every pair of jeans you owned."

By that point, the devil has usually fled, and I am left looking for a nice, dry, fat-free, high-fiber bran muffin. But I am not happy. Quite the contrary—I feel deprived.

That's how I used to feel before I understood the meaning of chastity—when I was following friends' and relatives' advice to "stop looking."

I knew some of the negative reasons for forgoing dates with men who were out for casual sex—such encounters would make me feel used and leave me lonelier than before—but I lacked positive reasons.

To lose weight without feeling deprived takes more than just listening to the warnings of the angel on my shoulder. It takes a positive vision. I have to imagine how I'll look and feel far into the future—not just tomorrow but tomorrow and tomorrow and tomorrow. I have to widen my perspective and see the cumulative effect of temptation: every time I give in, it wears down my resistance, but every time I resist, I grow stronger.

The tomorrow principle requires that vision to be able to see how chastity will help me become the strong, sensitive, confident woman I so long to be. I hate acting out of desperation, feeling as if I have to give of myself physically because it's the only way to reach a man emotionally. And I hate feeling so lonely that I have to take caresses and kisses from a man who essentially views me as a piece of meat—a rare and attractive piece of meat, deserving of the highest respect, but meat nonetheless. I long with all my heart to be able to look beyond my immediate desires, conducting myself with the grace and wisdom that will ultimately bring me fulfillment not just for a night but for a lifetime.

◆ ◆ ◆

The value of the tomorrow principle became real to me late one night in the spring of 2002, as I was preparing to leave a party in a Brooklyn apartment. The host, Steve, was a singer and songwriter I'd known for years, though never very well. We'd long had a mild flirtation going, but nothing had come of it because we didn't really have much in common other than physical attraction. So I was caught off guard when he asked if I'd like to stay the night.

My first thought was a vision of the long, scary, late-night subway ride home, contrasted with the appeal of sharing Steve's bed. I imagined the easy camaraderie we would share, the breaking down of boundaries, and the fleeting romantic moments—all those things that I really looked forward to in casual encounters. It was not so much a sexual fantasy as a fantasy of hormonal highs and a kind of intimacy. In my heart, I knew that whatever might transpire would not be true intimacy—more like an empty pantomime—but at least it would provide a brief distraction from loneliness.

As my mind ran through the possible scenarios, I remembered that my spiritual situation had changed since the last time I'd received such an offer. I was a baby Christian now, still wet behind the ears, and I knew I wanted my life to reflect my faith. But what made me tell Steve no wasn't the force of conviction. It was another vision that flashed through my brain, sharper than the first—as though it had actually happened.

In that vision, I saw myself and Steve the next morning, at a diner—not a shiny reproduction of a 1950s hangout but a bona fide old-fashioned greasy spoon in his neighborhood. I was wearing the same jeans and purple velvet blouse I had worn to the party. My hair was still a little wet from showering, and it was poking out in all the wrong directions (it doesn't hold up well when I don't use conditioner).

We were having breakfast and attempting to keep our conversation light, as if we'd just happened to run into each other at ten o'clock on a Sunday morning. In front of me was the same morning meal I always order at a New York diner: poached eggs on dry rye toast, no potatoes, and coffee with skim milk.

The image was pathetic.

Just the idea of one more uncomfortable morning-after breakfast, my loveless partner oozing with "respect"—that is, what qualifies as respect in the casual-dating world ("I'll still respect you")—was more than I could bear.

But the vision also had a more insidious quality, which I can describe only as grotesque. Here I was, so choosy that I insisted on four different specifications for my diner breakfast. Yet, I couldn't hold out for the one man with whom I could share every breakfast for the rest of my life?

The Shirelles' "Will You Love Me Tomorrow" suggests that a night of sex sans marital vows is redeemed if the couple declares after the fact that they love each other. The concept is a standby in popular culture; think, or rather, don't think, of all the films where a prostitute and client become a real couple. People buy into such a fantasy because they want to believe that objectifying someone else is excusable.

Yet, in my vision of breakfast with Steve, even if he suddenly professed his undying love as I bit into my egg on toast, it wouldn't change the decision I'd made the night before: to sleep with him not because I loved him but just because I could. Even if I wound up loving him back, it wouldn't change the fact that twelve hours earlier, I'd intended to use him and be used.

If we ever got married, that would be our story: we were acquainted without being good friends, "hooked up" one night after having a few drinks, and fell in love. Somehow, I don't think that's a recipe for a lasting marriage. If having sex with me were enough to make my husband fall in love, he might go on to have sex with another woman and fall in love with her too. Likewise, if I as his wife were that easily won over, I'd be liable to run off with the pizza deliveryman.

But that's silly. I'm not like that, and I knew even while imagining it that I would be no more likely to fall in love with Steve after sex than I was at that moment. I would, however, feel more attached to him, even if it wasn't love. Sexual intercourse would do that to me whether I wanted it to or not; it's part of how I'm wired as a woman. That sense of attachment would make the separation after breakfast that much harder.

Once that image entered my mind, the choice was clear.

I thanked Steve for a lovely party and left. Somewhere during the journey from the midnight Brooklyn streets to my New Jersey apartment, I think I cried. Turning down intimacy—even the wrong kind—can hit hard when you're coming home to an empty place.

But I don't regret it, and I've lived by the tomorrow principle ever since.

If you have to ask someone if he'll still love you tomorrow, then he doesn't love you tonight.

2

WHY IT'S EASY TO BLAME
MOM AND DAD
(AND WHY YOU SHOULDN'T)

I invite you to think back upon your childhood for a moment. Did you grow up having a mother and father who loved each other and stayed married to each other as long as they lived? Was there no time when you felt unloved or unwanted? Were you never abused, rejected, unprotected, or intentionally exposed to things that a child should not experience (such as pornography, adult nudity, or graphic sex talk)?

If your young life was so perfect that all of the above applies, congratulations! You can skip to the next chapter. While you are at it, please say a prayer for the 99.9 percent of readers who will be reading on.

Granted, the 99.9 percent figure is a (very) unofficial estimate, but based on my experience over the past couple of years since I began writing and speaking on healing from childhood trauma, I do not think it is very far off. The world is full of walking wounded, and the pews on Sunday are no different.

Looking back at my first few years of trying to live chastely, I realize that many of the difficulties I faced—including loneliness, proneness to sexual fantasies, and an unhealthy desire for affirmation from men—were complicated by childhood wounds that I had failed to address. Only when I began to be honest with myself, recognizing how I had allowed those childhood wounds to shape my adult identity, did I find healing, strength, and a way toward forgiveness.

◆ ◆ ◆

I was five when my parents separated; they divorced a year later. My mother was given custody of my older sister and me, and my father had visitation on weekends. I think that, as with many parents during the divorce boom of the 1970s, they were intent on having a "good" divorce. They believed that if they did not fight over custody and if they treated one another with respect (however grudging), my sister and I would make it through their split with minimal emotional damage.

Despite their efforts to put on a brave face, it was obvious to me that my parents retained hurt feelings toward each other. Before I reached second grade, I knew more than kids should know about their parents' interpersonal relations: Mom thought Dad was shallow; Dad thought Mom was flighty.

Although neither of them wanted to hurt me, the effect was that I felt pressured to take sides. Mom would point out when Dad would slight me in some way, like when he failed to come to my school recitals (as if I didn't notice), while Dad would make a remark if Mom dressed me in shabby clothes. (When I reported my father's complaints to my mother, she would respond that he should use his superior paycheck to buy me a new outfit.)

My parents' feeding me negative opinions of each other led me to form prejudices against them that I had to work to overcome, but the most profound effect of their placing me in the midst of their emotional drama was that they made me prematurely aware of grown-up dysfunction. Without meaning to do so, they created a cynic.

◆ ◆ ◆

There was another effect of my parents' split, one that I avoided mentioning in the original edition of this book because I was not yet ready to discuss it publicly. As I have since related in *My Peace I Give You*, once my father was no longer present to protect me, I suffered sexual abuse.

The first time I was victimized was during my parents' separation by a janitor at the temple my family attended. He told me to keep it a secret. It took courage for me to tell my mother, because I feared she would tell me I had done something wrong.

The fear proved true. I remember my mother exclaiming, aghast, "How could you let him do that?"[1]

I could not give an acceptable answer. It is hard to respond to that kind of question at any age and impossible when you are just entering first grade.

Although my mother reported the abuse to the temple's rabbi (who did not believe me), she never told my father. For my part, given the way my mother had reacted to the news, I certainly wasn't about to tell him. The result was that I internalized misplaced guilt and shame. For the rest of my childhood, I felt "dirty." The feeling arose not because my family was in any way prudish about sex (they weren't), but because I was made to feel responsible for actions that had personally revolted me even while they were taking place. In my child's mind, I had "let" a bad man use me.

Sexual predators normally seek out children who are already vulnerable. The misplaced guilt I carried, along with not having my father's protection at home, made me an easy target. I remember one of my mother's boyfriends abusing me at home, in my mother's presence. More than that, I remember the environment at my mother's home as being sexually porous. I don't recall clear boundaries. I was not well-shielded from adults who engaged in graphic talk about sex, swore, and got drunk, high, or nude.

My father knew very little about this. He remarried soon after the divorce, and when I saw him on weekends, he did not want to know what was going on inside my mother's home. A few years later, when I was nine, he and my stepmother moved thousands of miles away. The physical distance between us was matched by emotional distance; our meetings and conversations were few and (mostly) brief.

I do not recall any particularly meaningful father/daughter talks from that time. Dad did not speak to me about what makes for a healthy relationship. It was understood that if I had anything to discuss about sex, my mother was the one to ask.

So, in the manner of hostages who suffer "Stockholm syndrome," which causes them to feel dependent upon their kidnappers, I became psychologically dependent, even enmeshed, with my mother—my one confidante, the only person who had the power to protect me. This co-identification, as well as the lack of boundaries at home, led me to have a disturbingly close perspective on my mother's efforts to find a man who would love her.

If there are any single parents reading this, here is the best advice I can give you on raising your children to be chaste: never have a lover sleep over who is not your spouse, and never leave your children for the night in order to sleep at your lover's home. Both of my parents, even after their divorce, held up marriage as an ideal. They each told me as a child that they hoped I would one day fall in love and get married, but all the words in the world mean nothing if you do not give your children a sincere and living witness that what we do with God's gift of sexuality matters.[2]

◆ ◆ ◆

As a teenager, feeling inside like a vulnerable, unprotected child, I sought to protect myself by projecting a false self. I dressed provocatively, used sexual language in everyday conversation, and prided myself on being sexually aggressive. It was my way of trying to have control. I thought that if men were going to use me anyway, I could at least have some control over how they did so. Without consciously being aware, I had effectively entered into a vicious cycle in which, having been a victim of predators, I was advertising my insecurity and low self-image—and so becoming an easy target for men who *did* in fact want to use me.

Ultimately, what saved me from self-destruction was the grace of conversion, as I'll relate in the next chapter. But there were also two important things that led me to be open to that grace, and both of them involved changes in my parents' behavior.

First, when I was sixteen, my mother experienced her own conversion, which led her to enter the Catholic Church and change her way of life. Although I bore no admiration for her Catholicity, I admired the self-control my mother displayed in striving to live according to her newfound faith. What I did not know was that she was praying fervently through the intercession of St. Monica that I would find my way into the Church as did Monica's son, St. Augustine.

Second, when I was in my late twenties, my relationship with my father was transformed for the better, thanks to an intervention by my stepmother. This brave woman took the initiative to urge my father to examine his relationships with his children. He was surprised to learn that I did not feel he was emotionally involved in my life—and that I had always felt his love was conditional.

Upon realizing that his communications with me over the years had failed to convey the love he felt, my father began to actively take an interest in my well-being. He would listen when I told him about the things in my life that were important to me. No longer did I feel he was only interested in my measurable accomplishments. He cared about more than what I did; he cared about who I was.

I am convinced that my journey into the Church was jump-started by witnessing each of my parents become better people, and especially by the healing that took place in my relationship with my father. Once he began to reach out to me in a meaningful way, it became harder for me to convince myself that men cared only about what I could give them. Cynicism was starting to get old.

◆ ◆ ◆

Whether your parents influenced you in a positive way or you are trying to overcome your upbringing, your feelings about them will affect you as you work to change your life. If you are beginning your journey toward living chastely, now is a good time to reflect on the lessons you ought to retain from them and the lessons you had best discard. Here are a few things to think about while considering where you came from and where you're going:

- **Instead of repeating your parents' mistakes, you can learn from them.** Knowledge is power. What negative messages did you receive as a child about your attractiveness, your intelligence, or the meaning of marriage and sexual union? The more you understand how you were influenced by those messages, the more you will be able to view them from an older, wiser, and more objective perspective.

For example, when I was growing up, my mother weighed herself every day and would then verbalize how she felt about what the scale showed: happy if she had lost weight, disappointed if she hadn't. Since I identified with her in an unhealthy manner, I grew up to be extremely self-conscious about my own weight.

At a certain point in my adult life, I came to realize that such self-consciousness was a harmful holdover from a time when I lacked a solid sense of identity. If I wanted to be healthy and keep my weight down, there were ways to do it besides letting my self-image depend on what the scale said on a given morning. So I made the conscious decision to put away the scale and save my weigh-ins for doctor checkups, concentrating instead on making sure I fit into my favorite clothes. Doing so was liberating. It enabled me to affirm in a constructive way that I was not my mother; I was my own woman.

- **Someone was looking out for you, whether you wanted them to or not.** Chances are that at some point during your childhood, Mom or Dad sat you down and tried to tell you something to help you get through life. What messages did your parents give you that ring true in your mature experience? Perhaps a parent tried to give you a sound moral message and you discounted it because it was said in a manner that annoyed you, or because you simply weren't interested. Doesn't it feel good now to realize that one of your parents cared enough about you to try, however awkwardly, to steer you on the right path? Now is as good a time as any to thank him or her—and to say you're sorry you didn't listen before.

- **When all is said and done, your parents are human beings with human foibles.** One of the best spiritual gifts one receives in adulthood is the ability to see one's parents as people. My mother often asks me how I would feel to have children as old as my sister and I were when she was my age. I have to admit, I can't imagine. Not until recently did I come to understand what human sexual love is for. The idea of having to explain it to kids is unfathomable. (It is hard enough explaining it to adults.) Gaining a wider perspective is essential if you're going to . . .
- **Forgive your parents.** Forgiveness is crucial because your parents are not getting any younger, and neither are you—and also because God says so.[3] Most important, every effort you make to forgive your parents will bring you healing and strength for the journey ahead.

3

MY JOURNEY HOME (TO ROME)

I was speaking recently with an unmarried female friend who was feeling lonely, and she brought up an utterance that St. Bernadette reported during the apparitions at Lourdes, when Mary said she could promise Bernadette happiness not in this world but only in the next.[1]

My friend, in her disillusionment, took Mary's message to mean that she herself was not meant to have happiness in this world.

At the time, I responded as a friend would, telling her I knew God had a plan for her, a plan for her well-being and not for evil, to give her a future and a hope (see Jer 29:11). Afterward I realized I could have challenged her interpretation of the apparition. Mary is, after all, Our Lady of Hope. Granted, in apparitions that have been approved by the Church, including Lourdes, she urges the faithful to penance. But she always points to healing in Christ—healing that brings joy in this life. Lourdes didn't receive its reputation as one of the world's top pilgrimage sites by sending people home depressed.

So, what *did* Mary mean in speaking to Bernadette? By promising happiness only in heaven, was she condemning the French teenager to a life of meaninglessness?

That is not what Bernadette thought. To gain an idea of how she understood Mary's words, we can look at a letter written in 1863, fifteen years after the Lourdes apparitions, when she was a religious sister. The author of the letter was Father C. Alix, a priest who had given her spiritual direction. His words meant so much to Bernadette that, ten years after receiving the letter, she transcribed it in her own hand so as to have a fresh copy of the words she had read and reread so many times.

In the letter, Father Alix offered Bernadette "a few thoughts on holiness" that he hoped would provide food for her meditations. Among the advice he gives, one point reads as though he were interpreting Mary's promise to her of happiness in heaven: "Give the appearance of living on earth as long as it pleases God to leave you here, but in reality, live in Heaven in your thoughts, your emotions, and your desires."[2]

The priest's advice brings out the beauty of Mary's affirmation that Bernadette would have happiness in the next world, and does so by pointing to the same truth we read in the *Catechism of the Catholic Church*: "Our participation in the Eucharist already gives us a foretaste of Christ's transfiguration of our bodies" (CCC 1000).

I may yet have a mortal body and have to struggle to avoid sin, and I may, like the Psalmist, feel like crying out, "When can I enter and see the face of God?" (Ps 42:3). Even so, now that I am a Catholic sharing in the sacramental life of the Church, heaven is no longer an alien and faraway place. Heaven is a *living reality*. Those in a state of grace, even in this life, find themselves at its leading edge.

Unlike Bernadette, I am no visionary. But as I reflect upon the events that led to my conversion, certain experiences—some painful and some joyful—reveal themselves in retrospect to have been the beginning of a divine in-breaking.

♦ ♦ ♦

It seemed as though I was always running, a born escapist.

Some of my earliest memories are of my parents' arguing. Perhaps that is why I learned to read before I even started school—absorbing the letters and sounds as I lost myself in "Sesame Street." From then on, when Mom and Dad's harsh rebukes to one another sounded in my ears, I had a way out. I could turn off the television, go to my room, shut the door, open a book, and enter another world.

My favorites were stories such as Lewis Carroll's *Alice's Adventures in Wonderland* and *Through the Looking-Glass*. Reading them, I could imagine myself in the place of the bright little girl whose journeys into the unknown began with flight from everyday life.

From the Alice books, I graduated to C. S. Lewis's *The Lion, the Witch, and the Wardrobe*. With it, I received new food for my imagination—and a strange new edge to my longing to escape, one that I did not quite understand.

As with *Through the Looking-Glass*, the plot of Lewis's fantasy turned upon a piece of ordinary household furniture becoming a gateway to a fantastic new dimension. But the image of the double-doored wardrobe as mystical portal was familiar in a personal, almost experiential way—one that was all the more mysterious because I couldn't put my finger on where I had seen it before.

♦ ♦ ♦

After my parents' divorce, my mother moved my sister and me from our beautiful house on the bay in Galveston, Texas, into an apartment across town that had stucco walls and what Mom joked were cockroach electoral conventions on the ceiling. In place of our rather staid former neighbors was a steady trickle of colorful and sweaty houseguests: artists, shipbuilders, yoga fanatics, and small-town actresses. When they broke out the jug bottle of Paul Masson white wine, I would close my bedroom door in a vain attempt to shut out the marijuana smoke, the childish giggling, and the ironic strains of my mother's favorite song crackling over the phonograph—Crosby, Stills, Nash and Young's "Teach Your Children."

I would open a book and fly away.

As long as I had something to read, I was well behaved, which was why Mom let me take my books to temple services on Friday nights. She retained enough of a connection to her Jewish faith to instill the religion in my sister and me, even though she herself had taken to spending her mornings at the ashram.

I didn't spend too much time in reading during services. I couldn't; there was too much going on, especially when the Torah section of the service began. The veil of the ark in the wall behind the pulpit would be parted, and the doors behind it opened to reveal the scroll containing the five books of Moses, covered in an embroidered velvet sheath that bore Hebrew lettering and the image of a crown. All in the sanctuary would stand and sing as the rabbi placed the bulky Torah in his arms so that it leaned on his shoulder as he processed it down the aisle and back. He carried it as delicately as if it were a baby. Until the day when I would become a *bat mitzvah* at thirteen and would read from the Torah before the entire congregation, that was the nearest I could approach the sacred scroll.

The Torah scroll's parchment, as with the holy mountain in Exodus, was sacred, not to be touched except by a special metal pointer, a *yad*. As the rabbi passed my aisle, I would lean over, as my mother had instructed me, touching the Torah's cover with my prayer book and then kissing the book with solemn devotion.

Then the Torah would be uncovered and placed on a table in the middle of the pulpit; the week's scripture was read, and we all stood and sang as the scroll was returned to its place in the ark, a shuttered cabinet at the center of the wall behind the pulpit. I had one last glimpse of the scroll as it stood majestically in its home; then the ark's doors were shut, its veil closed, and the sanctuary resumed its normal outlines, its aura of holiness diminished.

I was always sorry to see the Torah disappear from sight, though I couldn't have told you why. Now I realize it was because I longed for the presence of God.

◆ ◆ ◆

In my twenties, I rarely escaped into books, preferring to lose myself in rock music, which I wrote about for magazines and websites. But in December 1995, when a rock musician I was interviewing by phone told me he was reading a novel by an author I had never heard of, I decided to read it myself so I might have something to talk about with him the next time he was in town.

The novel, by G. K. Chesterton, had the mysterious title *The Man Who Was Thursday*. Written in 1907, it begins with an impromptu debate in a London park between two poets. One is a poet of anarchism and revolution. The other calls himself "a poet of law, a poet of order; . . . a poet of respectability."

It was easy to choose which character's side to take. I longed to be "creative"—and, as with Chesterton's revolutionary poet, I believed creativity was defined by rebellion. This was the time when I was projecting an aggressive, hypersexualized false self—trying to protect myself from getting hurt but doing so in a way that only advertised my insecurity.

So, reading *The Man Who Was Thursday*, I rooted for the revolutionary—until a line spoken by his adversary jumped out at me. In response to the revolutionary's claim that "the poet delights in disorder only," the "poet of order" insists to the contrary: "The most poetical thing in the world is not being sick."

The words were meant to be shocking, and they were—shocking enough to force me to pause and let the light of grace enter in. At that moment, I desired with all my heart to experience healing, to have my life ordered from the top down, and to know the *poetry* of not being sick.

◆ ◆ ◆

In *My Peace I Give You*, I reflect on my Baptism at a Protestant church and the movements of grace through which I was led to discover the truth of the Catholic faith. Right now, I am thinking about the moment on Holy Thursday, 2006, when the running stopped. A newly professed Catholic, I received the Body and Blood of Christ for the first time.

Gazing upon the tabernacle, my thoughts went back to my earliest experience of the presence of holiness—that is, a sense of the sacred emanating from a *place* and not a person I could see.

The memories of my childhood fascination with the ark came back to me. They still return whenever I gaze at what is, for Catholics, the Holy of Holies, where the Real Presence of the Lord—his eucharistic body—is reserved. The Catholic Church, as well as each individual church, is the *porta caeli*, the true "gate of heaven" that was prefigured in the Old Testament (Gn 28:17).

That *porta* truly is the portal to another world. When I gaze upon the veil of the tabernacle, like Alice musing over the looking glass, I imagine that the other side of it extends into forever. And, like her, I wish I could be absorbed into it while remaining myself.

◆ ◆ ◆

In fact, the forever curious protagonist of Carroll's tales, even when propelled into the most fantastic surroundings, does remain the same little girl. John Tenniel's original illustrations to *Through the Looking-Glass* show that Alice, in crossing to the other side of the mirror, retains her original dimensions; she does not change into a mirror image of herself.

Alice's retention of her original form is accentuated by the fact that, unlike in *Alice's Adventures in Wonderland*, in which she is almost continually eating or drinking, she does not consume a single thing in "Looking-Glass world." She tries many times, but the foodstuffs come alive, and as the Red Queen reminds her, "it isn't etiquette to cut anyone you've been introduced to." All of this makes perfect sense, since, as *Annotated Alice* author Martin Gardner observes, looking-glass food would have been poisonous to someone from the other side; its isotopes would be reversed.[3]

It is there that the analogy of the tabernacle to a "Looking-Glass-style" gateway breaks down, because I *can* eat the food from the other side—the *panis angelicus*, "bread of angels"—and, far from destroying my substance, it perfects it, bringing it closer to being capable of existing in heaven.

◆ ◆ ◆

Once I entered the Church, I knew I was home; there was nowhere else to go. If there was any healing to be found, it had to be there. But when I tried to find healing for my childhood wounds through the means available to me in faith, I faced unexpected challenges.

The most disturbing obstacle arose when a Catholic therapist, who had been recommended to me by a friend, told me that he couldn't really help me unless I was willing to revisit every single painful memory and "invite Jesus in." I refused to do so, fearing that reliving the abuse of my childhood would be too much to bear. (Later, I found out the therapist's "PhD" was from a diploma mill, teaching me the value of the old saying "Trust but verify.")

Over time, as I learned what the Church teaches about suffering, I came to see how, as the Second Vatican Council says, "[through] Christ and in Christ, the riddles of sorrow and death grow meaningful."[4] Whatever pain I had in the moment could, I knew, become part of my daily offering to God, as I endured it in union with Jesus' Passion.[5] But I remained in a kind of mourning over what I saw as the "wasted" pain of my past—the sufferings I endured before becoming reborn in Christ.

So it was, one day in August 2010, that I found myself before the tabernacle with an unspoken prayer. I was in the midst of an eight-day stay at a retreat house in Ann Arbor, Michigan, my first time praying the Spiritual Exercises of St. Ignatius. The retreat director, Father Dennis Brown, O.M.V., had assigned me to meditate that afternoon upon St. Ignatius of Loyola's reflections on Jesus' Passion, so I went to the house's small chapel and began to pray before the tabernacle. My childhood pain was in the background of my thoughts, as it always was, but I was trying to think of Jesus and not myself.

That is when it happened.

As I prayed, I saw with my mind's eye the Eucharist, as though it were at the center of a bicycle-wheel shape, all made of light. The wheel's spokes reached out to all the earth, taking up everything and everyone in its embrace and drawing it all back to the center—back to the Eucharist.

At that moment, I realized for the first time that, whereas God could not change my past, he had done something infinitely better. He had changed *me*, by making me his beloved daughter in Christ.

After all, what is the past? It no longer exists, except inasmuch as it is part of what makes us who we are today. Contemplating the light of the "Sun of Righteousness" (Mal 4:2 RSV), I understood that, when I am really present for

Christ as he is really present for me in the Eucharist, his healing rays enter into every dark crevice of my heart. It is as though Jesus' Precious Blood bleeds back into my past, making even my most painful times part of a beautiful story—beautiful not because the evil was good (for evil can never be good) but because it ends with me belonging to him.[6]

So, I gaze today upon the tabernacle, and I no longer want to escape from my world. I want to pursue Jesus into his.

4

THE FIRST CUT IS THE DEEPEST

When I made the decision to enter into full communion with the Catholic Church, I had grand visions of my first confession. If St. Ignatius Loyola's first confession after his conversion of life took three whole days, surely mine would at least require meals to be sent in.

But it was not to be. The Polish Dominican priest who guided my catechesis informed me that, since the Church recognized the Baptism I had received six years before, I only needed only to confess sins committed since Baptism.

So, given that my Baptism had spurred me to conversion of life, my first confession was much briefer than I expected—briefer, in fact, than many that I've made since (not that my sins have gotten worse but rather that I've become more conscious of them). To be truthful, I was relieved. The glamour of enumerating past transgressions fades when you begin to realize that the priest is not there to be impressed; he is there to be the human instrument of the divine reconciliation Christ won for you with his blood.

Looking back, I recognize that day as the beginning of my journey to a greater sensitivity to sin.

◆ ◆ ◆

As a new convert to Catholicism, even though I loved the writings of G. K. Chesterton, I could not relate to the response that the great British author gave to those who asked why he entered the Church: "To get rid of my sins."[1] I had been Protestant for nearly five years when I chose to become Catholic, and during that time I believed that God forgave my sins whenever I repented, with no need for an intermediary. It had never occurred to me that reconciliation with God in Christ could not be complete unless I also sought to be reconciled with the Church, through which Christ remains present on earth.

Until I made my first confession, my mental concept of sin extended primarily to external actions, and especially sexual transgressions. Over time, especially once I started to get into the rhythm of confessing regularly, I grew increasingly conscious that those external actions didn't just spring out of nowhere.

First, I noticed that my outward sexual sins had their origins in thoughts and fantasies. When I tried to follow those thoughts and fantasies back to their source, I found a tangle of wrong ideas and dark thoughts about myself and others, which played themselves out not only in sexual sins but also in other sins that had long festered below my conscious radar.

Slowly, with the help of good confessors, it became clear that, when I lusted after a man, the real problem might not be lust so much as envy ("the woman who has him doesn't deserve him"), pride ("I deserve him"), or resentment ("how dare he not notice me"). It could even be a sin against the Love Commandment: failing to love God enough to trust that he has a plan for me.[2]

You might think that such growing sensitivity to sin could make a person feel hopeless, even despair. But the truth is, while sinful habits themselves are painful, it actually feels *good* to know where these sins are coming from. I think that is why Venerable Fulton J. Sheen spent so much effort urging people to consider spending time in the confessional before spending money on therapy.[3]

There is no question that some people need professional help for reasons not primarily related to spiritual needs—for example, those who suffer from a chemical imbalance, or who are tempted to harm themselves or others. But I think most people who seek therapy simply want to gain more control over their lives by learning why they are unhappy and what they can do about it. That's where the Sacrament of Reconciliation comes in.

While it's no sin to be unhappy, the fact that there is any unhappiness in the world is due to sin. Whatever makes me unhappy is due to sins I commit, sins committed against me, or the general state of brokenness resulting from original sin.

The Sacrament of Reconciliation helps me deal with the effects of sin in all its facets. Where my own sins are concerned, sacramental confession does more than erase them. It leads me to examine where my sinful impulses are coming from and gives me the grace to fight those impulses when they reappear. When given a clearer awareness of those impulses and improved control over them, I can better deal with the pain of being sinned against, as well as the sad effects of original sin (human frailty, sickness, and death).

It was the Sacrament of Reconciliation that led me to examine my past more deeply and to discover the roots of my temptations. With reflection, I came to see that I lost my innocence well before I lost my virginity. I lost it when I learned that it was possible to separate sexual sensation from love.

◆ ◆ ◆

My brief relationship with my first boyfriend set the stage for my loss of innocence.

When I was fifteen and despairing of finding a boyfriend at my suburban high school who shared my offbeat interests (which then included punk rock and various kinds of social rebellion), my mom let me go on a weekend teen retreat at a Unitarian church. There I met a brainy guy named Gavin, who although just a year older than me, seemed far more independent and experienced.

Gavin was immersed in the hard-core punk scene, meaning he would go to nightclubs where dancing was replaced by "moshing"—a bizarre, testosterone-fueled ritual in which young men would slam their bodies against one another to the sound of live "music" consisting of incomprehensible shouts, grating guitars, throbbing bass lines, and mile-a-minute drums. Yet, while his social environment was riddled with violence and substance abuse, Gavin himself was gentle and avoided excess. In that way, he fit my teenage ideal—one that I think is shared by many young women who have suffered abuse or neglect—of a "bad boy" who is not *really* bad.

One night, after we had been dating about three weeks and had exchanged just a few quick kisses during that time, Gavin and I went to an all-ages punk concert in Lower Manhattan. I unfortunately proved to be a real drag, because I had yet to grasp that one does not go to a hardcore concert unless one is willing to get stomped on. And that is exactly what happened: a hardy young male jumped off the rafters and kicked my head on his way down. Perhaps the head kick was really meant as some sort of hardcore sign of camaraderie, but I took it badly—running out of the nightclub in tears.

Gavin followed me out. He didn't say much to comfort me—it was obvious to him that I should have known what I was in for—but I managed to stop crying. I had to leave soon anyway because my mom was going to pick me up, so he and I filled the rest of our time together with a walk around the block, a deserted place of warehouses and parking lots.

We stopped to lean against a metal barrier, and Gavin started kissing me. I was self-conscious because I'd only kissed a couple of boys before, and those were boys who didn't know what they were doing. From the way he kissed, it was clear he knew what he was doing, and I wasn't sure how to handle this new stage of our relationship.

Back then, I didn't believe in waiting until marriage. As I shared in chapter 2, I grew up in a liberal household; neither of my parents wanted to seem like prudes. It was understood that I would engage in sexual intercourse when I was ready, whether married or not, but I did have from childhood a deep desire to wait until I was really and truly "in love"—whatever that meant.

I don't recall telling Gavin that I wanted to wait to have sex until I was really in love, but he must have picked up on it. At least, that was my guess when I thought afterward about what transpired between us on that dark street. All I knew was that after I got into my mom's car, I never saw him again. He stopped calling me and stopped returning my calls. I guessed I had moved too slowly for him; he was experienced, after all.

As the months went by and I kept rehashing my few dates with Gavin in my head, the message was clear: even if I was going to save sex for when I was finally in love, I had to get more experience. I would show my dream man that I wasn't uptight. It was the only way to keep him interested until the magic moment when everything would fall into place.

◆ ◆ ◆

In the fall of my senior year of high school, when I was sixteen (having skipped a year in my haste to graduate), I hopped a train to visit a man I'll call Travis, at his East Village apartment.

Travis was a magazine writer and music-business professional originally from Nebraska—and twice my age. Two years earlier, I had phoned the editor of an underground entertainment magazine for which he wrote. I was fascinated with entertainment journalism and brazenly asked the editor if he would meet me and a few friends for lunch sometime. The editor—no doubt bemused to get a phone call from a fourteen-year-old girl in New Jersey—did meet us, and he brought Travis along.

I don't know what motivated me to visit Travis on that day two years after our meeting, or why it took me so long to make the trip. Since our lunch, we had occasionally exchanged correspondence. I was impressed that a man I considered important took an interest in me. To me, there was nothing more exciting than working for a major recorded-music company and writing magazine articles on music and film. I was eager to learn about all the seemingly important things that were absent from my suburban existence, and I wanted to learn from Travis.

He also had another dimension that I found intriguing, in an edgy kind of way: on the side, he wrote for pornographic magazines. I wasn't a fan of pornography and knew there were good feminist reasons to oppose it. On my way to see him, after arriving in Manhattan via underground rail, I passed the woman from Feminists Fighting Pornography who stood every Saturday at a table at Broadway and Eighth Street, shouting in her thick New York accent, "Women! Fight back! Sign the petition!" Beside her was a giant blowup of the notoriously offensive cover of *Hustler* magazine that showed a woman's legs sticking out of a meat grinder.

Despite my reservations, Travis's involvement with the pornography industry gave his corn-fed Nebraskan demeanor an air of danger. It added to the pleasant sense of rebelliousness that I already felt going into New York City by myself to see a much older man.

◆ ◆ ◆

The only place to sit in Travis's studio apartment was his king-size bed. We made small talk for a while, bringing each other up to speed on what had happened in our lives during the two years since the lunch we'd shared when I was fourteen. I told him I had seen a music video by Suzanne Vega, a singer whose career he had helped. Finally—and I must have known this would happen—he asked if he could kiss me.

I knew for certain that I was attracted to men. More than that, I was capable of being overwhelmingly attracted, with a crush so intense that it virtually blinded me and made me swoon.

I did not feel that way with Travis, but neither was I repelled by him.

He was . . . there. There was nothing particularly unattractive about him. And that, combined with my lack of a crush on him, made him safe.

Ever since Gavin had dumped me, I had felt as though I was invisible to any man who sparked my interest. Looking at photos of myself from that time, I see that there was nothing off-putting about my appearance, but at the time I was convinced that I was unattractive. None of the boys I liked at school would have anything to do with me. There seemed to be some sort of "it" factor that I lacked.

Travis fed my ego when I was at my most vulnerable. If he found me attractive, chances were that someone else—someone I would be crazy about—would too. In the meantime, I thought, I could gain some experience with

him, so that boys I liked would no longer see me as goofy
or, worse, uptight.

But first came the uncertain moment when I told Travis that I was a virgin—and what's more, planned to stay
that way until I found "The One."

He assured me that he just wanted to "neck." Anytime
I wanted, I could just turn on the red lights.

I consented. Travis went to his collection of vinyl
record albums (this was before the advent of digital music)
and pulled out a recording from his youth, the Flamin'
Groovies' *Teenage Head*. He was taken with the idea of making out like a teenager.

◆ ◆ ◆

I visited Travis several more times that school year. During
that time, neither of us ever removed clothing or touched
each other under clothes. I was too quick with the red lights
for that—and he would always stop, as he had promised.

Not being really attracted to him, I viewed our sessions as opportunities to gain the experience I lacked. Only
my body was really with him; my mind was watching
the scene as if it was a TV show, while my emotions were
buried too deeply for me to realize how they were being
affected.

I told my mom that I was friends with Travis (I had
a hard time hiding anything from her, because we were
close), but didn't tell her we were more than friends. She
later told me that she knew, but she didn't push it. It was
around the time when she had just received Christian faith
and was beginning to integrate Gospel teachings into her
own life. While she was concerned for me, I think she was
uncomfortable at the thought of dictating chastity.

I had mixed feelings about what Travis and I were
doing. On the one hand, it gave me something exciting to
tell the girls I lunched with at my high school cafeteria.

They listened with interest even though they thought the idea of dating a thirty-two-year-old was kind of weird. On the other, it got to be boring after a while. I knew Travis wasn't "The One," and it was pointless to take things further. But I liked the feeling of being a grown-up: getting away for a secret rendezvous at a real downtown Manhattan apartment—not just a boy's parents' basement—and having a bit of suspense over how far things might go.

◆ ◆ ◆

By the spring semester of my freshman year of college, when I was seventeen, I had long since moved on from Travis, but we were still friendly. He invited me to a party celebrating the release of a book by a local cartoonist.

At the party, Travis greeted me warmly. He wanted me to meet the publisher of the marijuana lovers' magazine *High Times*. I wasn't into drugs, but when it came to meeting "fashionable" people, I wasn't picky.

As Travis brought me over to the publisher, he said, "Is it okay if I tell him about us? About how you used to come over, and we'd make out, and because you were a virgin, you'd put on the red lights?"

For a moment, I was thrown off balance. Was that a real question? Did the phrasing even leave me the option to say "no"? Catching my breath (and unable to think of a polite way to exit the conversation), I said, "Okay."

I would like to say that was a moment when I suppressed my conscience, but I'm not sure how much there was to suppress. A conscience isn't something that you receive in its completeness at birth and retain unchanged throughout life. You have to form it, taking the initiative to learn not just what *seems* good but also what truly is good.

Having been raised Jewish, I knew the Ten Commandments. I knew that my grandparents, and all previous generations of my family, believed that sexual contact—even "necking"—should be reserved for marriage. But I had not submitted myself to the authority of the Torah or to any authority other than my own desires. My conscience was based on feelings, and feelings, as we all know, can change.

Yet, even without believing there was reason to obey the Word of God, something within me rebelled at the faint realization that I had used Travis, and let myself be used. Only much later would I learn what it was: the natural law, the law instilled in us at our creation by virtue of our being human, which reveals the inherent dignity of every man and woman.

I never hated Travis for what he did to me. In his and my situational ethics of the time, he was a model of honesty and respect. But I think of what it meant to him, to be a jaded pornography writer getting an ego boost from telling people about his experience with a virgin, and it seems terribly sad. No, not sad—make that pathetic.

And I let him do it. That was how far gone I was. I had lost my innocence, and I wasn't even aware that I had lost it, or that there had been anything to lose.

◆ ◆ ◆

There are certain points in one's memory that remain frozen in time. They're like fault lines—a nexus between past and present—and one keeps returning to them. Reflecting now on the period of my life when I was sexually active, my mind keeps returning to those afternoons with Travis. That is to say, I think about how they affected my perspective and my life choices; I don't actually relive them. (I hope it's clear by now that, when it comes to experiences worth reliving, the Travis sessions rate somewhere between sitting in the dentist's chair and watching paint dry.) No, the experiences in that studio apartment on First Avenue stick in my mind because they represent a contradiction that is essential to sexual contact outside of the matrimonial bond. It's something that I don't think the purveyors of a "sex-positive" culture will ever understand. (I do think sex within marriage is positive, but I'm referring to the views of those who take it beyond that context.)

From the sex-positive perspective, the Travis sessions were perfect "outercourse," as safe as safe could be. There was no genital contact.

However, from a Christian perspective, I was doing grave harm to my soul. It was truly unsafe sex. In a way, it was worse for me than actually having intercourse, because, had I done so—as bad as that would have been for me—I would have been more likely to realize what was going on.

As it was, I was like the person who takes a little poison each day and eventually becomes immune. Poison is never good for you; having the ability to ingest it without dying isn't a reason to do so on a regular basis.

In my case, I was learning to detach, to feel as though I could separate the physical actions of sex from its emotional consequences. I was also learning to be vicarious—to treat my partner as an object, to the point where my enjoyment consisted in seeing the effect I was having on him. It was a feeling of control, and it enabled me to further detach, so that I could move my partner without being moved myself.

My goal in all this was to have the excitement, ego boost, and physical companionship of sex—however temporary—without getting hurt. I always knew the separation would come and I'd be alone again. If I could limit how close I was to my partner in the first place, then the separation wouldn't be as pronounced, and I wouldn't crash.

❖ ❖ ❖

You lose your innocence when you learn to detach. You detach in order to protect yourself. When you protect yourself, sexual contact—(far from being a shared, other-directed experience of vowed love)—becomes an insular, narcissistic experience of insecurity.

The answer is to stop protecting yourself, and the only way to do that is to take yourself out of entanglements where you have to protect yourself. To truly connect with someone, you must allow yourself to be vulnerable. You can't be vulnerable if you're always having to ask yourself whether the man or woman you desire will be there to catch you when you fall.

These were the things I reflected upon as a new Catholic. When I did, I realized I could never regain my innocence, but I could regain my vulnerability.[4]

5

THE MEANING OF SEX

One day, when I was about eight years old, during a creative dramatics class where the teacher seemed willing to talk about anything, I blurted out a question that had been on my mind for a while: "How did sex get started?" The teacher, a woman in her twenties, was caught off guard. She hemmed and hawed for a moment, but I persisted: "How did the first men and women figure out how to have sex?" I still remember the teacher's attempt at an answer, because it was so odd. She came up with something vague about how perhaps the woman gave off a certain smell that drew the man over to have sex with her. It sounded sufficiently gross to throw me off track, but it wasn't really an answer.

Eight years later, when I was a senior in high school, my question changed to the far more common, "How do I start having sex?" But my experiences never taught me how sex got started—which is to say, why it got started. What is sex *for*?

We know that sexual intercourse is for reproduction. A strict materialist—that is, someone who believes that all thoughts may be traced to physical causes—might tell you that the feelings of intimacy human beings have during intercourse are simply biological trickery to get us to want to propagate the species. (Why biology would care whether we propagate the species is never explained.)

On the other hand, if you believe that what transpires between a man and a woman during intercourse has its source in something other than the couple's DNA, their upbringing, and what they had for lunch, then sex must have a function that goes beyond creating more people to have sex.

The Church has always had the same answer to the question of what sex is for, yet its answer could almost be called a best-kept secret in today's world. Granted, Catholic sexual teachings are often in the news, but if you think about it, the media rarely reports on what the Church teaches sex is for. Instead, it reports on what the Church teaches sex is *not* for. So we hear about the Church's opposition to homosexual acts, abortion, contraception, divorce, and sexual activity outside of marriage—in other words, against all the ideals of the so-called sexual revolution.

Although marriage and family began to fall under attack in the 1950s (as with Hugh Hefner's "*Playboy* philosophy"), traditional values remained the rule in the United States until the early 1960s, when the advent of the birth control pill enabled promiscuity to flourish. From there, sexual mores degenerated with astonishing speed into the hippie era, with its glorification of mind-altering drugs and "free love" (as opposed to the kind of love that cost money, apparently).

If the sexual revolution was a cultural earthquake, its epicenter was the "Summer of Love," the 1967 phenomenon that saw tens of thousands of young would-be hippies (many of them runaways) descend upon San Francisco expecting a new kind of freedom. Instead, they found a new kind of slavery, as guinea pigs in a kind of mass psychological experiment.

They thought that, by uniting their minds to drugs and their bodies to willing takers, they would overcome the superficial consumerism in which they had been raised and reach a higher spiritual level. Instead, all too often, being easy prey for pushers and sexual predators, they themselves became objects of consumption, being used and abused—or, worse still, they succumbed to the temptation to use and abuse others.

As the Summer of Love wound down, even the prime movers of San Francisco's hippie scene were disgusted at what their movement had become. Some of them staged a "Death of Hippie" ceremony, complete with a fake coffin.

Although the media exposed the crime, victimization, drug overdoses, and mindless conformity that plagued the sixties counterculture, one aspect of the hippie movement that never lost its luster in popular culture was the sexual revolution. A male journalist writing in 2007, when the media was celebrating the Summer of Love's fortieth anniversary, represented the common opinion as he gushed that the era's "lingering contribution" was "the freedom to choose one's own sexual path through life."[1]

That, my friend, is where I believe the secular mindset goes off the rails.

We read the words "freedom to choose one's own . . . path through life," and they go down so smoothly, so easily. Of *course* we should have the freedom to choose our path through life! It's the American way, and even the religious among us have to admit it is the Gospel truth. In the words of St. Paul, "For freedom Christ has set us free" (Gal 5:1 RSV).

Fair enough! But what, pray tell, can it possibly mean to have "the freedom to choose one's own *sexual* path through life"? Does it mean choosing whether and with whom to have sex, and when one wants to have sex?

If the journalist's argument is that the sexual revolution gave women some new kind of liberation that benefited them, then his image of choosing "one's sexual path through life" is particularly inapt. Making a path implies cutting through obstacles, calling to mind the peculiarly macho image of a sword slashing its way through foliage, leaving a path of destruction.

In that sense, come to think of it, the image is unintentionally very apt indeed. For the unbridled sexual aggression unleashed during the Summer of Love did leave a path of bodies strewn in its wake, via ballooning rates of sexually transmitted disease, abortion, divorce, and sexual abuse. But while San Francisco did its best to bury its reputation for squalor via its "Death of Hippie" ceremony, the hippies' fatally flawed ideal of sexual liberation refused to die. Like a zombie invasion, it infected the entire culture—spreading the lie that individuals could find true happiness only if they were willing to separate sexual activity from marriage and the possibility of procreation.

Because the lie at the base of the sexual revolution conflicts directly with the Church's defense of the divine design for human sexuality, opponents of Catholic teaching commonly accuse the Church of being narrowly focused upon "pelvic issues." It's wise, I think, to look carefully at the source of such an accusation. When secular culture insists true freedom is a life centered not upon growing in love of God and neighbor but rather on forging a "sexual path," then who is really obsessed with "pelvic issues"?

Indeed, Catholic writer Eric Sammons does not seem far off when, writing about dissent within the Church, he asserts that Catholics who vociferously defy Church teachings effectively set up a "pelvic trinity": abortion, contraception, and homosexuality.

"This unholy trinity of issues are of course interrelated and they all revolve around our 'right' to engage in sexual activities with no consequences," Sammons observes. "But these issues go even deeper, as they touch [on] whether we have the right to define morality as we see fit, or if there is One above us who makes those determinations. Ultimately, it comes down to the question of who is in charge: us or God."[2]

Those who refuse to let their desires be "raised with Christ" (Col 3:1) end up trying to justify their sinful behavior by remaking God in their own image. They are the people whom the Venerable Archbishop Fulton J. Sheen likened to those who said of Jesus, "let him come down from the cross now, and we will believe in him" (Mt 27:42). Today, they say to the Church that Christ founded,

> "Come down from your belief in the sanctity of marriage." "Come down from your belief in the sacredness of life." "Come down from your belief; the truth is merely what is pleasing." "Come down from the Cross of sacrifice and we will believe."[3]

But, as Sammons says, "Christ through his Church has a better way."[4] Rather than bring himself down to our level, he is always calling us to rise up to his, embracing the Cross so that we might share in his divine life:

> [Instead] of wallowing in sin which harms the human person, the Church's sexual ethic frees one to live as God designed us to live. And failure to live up to this sexual ethic is never total: even when we fall, Christ always offers us the grace—through confession and the Eucharist—to get back up and try again.[5]

◆ ◆ ◆

All right, then, what *is* the Church's answer to the question of what sex is for? For starters, the Catholic faith, seeking always to view human nature from a divine perspective, tells us that human persons are defined not by what they do but by who they *are*. To put it another way, the citizen of the secular city says, "I desire, therefore I am. Only through getting what I want, when I want it, in the way I want it, can I be satisfied." The Catholic says, "I am a child of God in Christ, therefore I want God to order all my desires so that they lead upward to him. Only through wanting what God wants for me, when he chooses to grant it to me, and in the way he chooses to grant it to me, can I be truly happy."

So the Church says that finding the answer to the question of what sex is for means looking well beyond the pelvis: "It is the whole man and the whole mission to which he is called that must be considered: both its natural, earthly aspects and its supernatural, eternal aspects."[6]

Those words are from *Humanae Vitae*, the landmark 1968 encyclical by Pope Paul VI that boldly proclaimed, in the face of the "free love" movement, that human sexual love cannot be truly free unless it is total, faithful, and fruitful—in a word, *marital*. Married love is

> above all fully human, a compound of sense and spirit. It is not, then, merely a question of natural instinct or emotional drive. It is also, and above all, an act of the free will, whose trust is such that it is meant not only to survive the joys and sorrows of daily life, but also to grow, so that husband and wife become in a way one heart and one soul, and together attain their human fulfillment.[7]

Against this vision of marital love as "an act of the free will" based on "trust" that survives all hardships and unites spouses' very souls in an upward journey toward the vision of God in heaven, the secular claim that a man and woman can love "freely" outside marriage is seen clearly for the lie that it is. No matter how much I may love a man, if he and

I refuse to vow ourselves to one another before Christ's representative, if we refuse to let the Holy Spirit seal our bond for as long as we both shall live, I am not truly *free* to make a gift of self to him.

To understand what I mean, imagine you invite a friend out for his birthday so that you may give him a present. Your friend says, "Sure, you are free to give me a present. Just know that, no matter what it is, I will return it to you one day, probably when you least expect it. Our friendship may change, and I don't want to be responsible for your gift if it turns out we don't get along." Are you really free to give your friend a gift? Isn't there something seriously wrong with the friendship that your friend would feel such a lack of trust that he could not simply accept whatever good thing you seek to give him? How, then, can a relationship between a man and a woman that is more than friendship be truly free without the partners' vowed promise, in the sight of God, to "generously share everything, allowing no unreasonable exceptions and not thinking solely of their own convenience"?[8]

St. John Paul II, early in his pontificate, saw the need for the Church to promote the "integral vision of man" given in *Humanae Vitae* as a counter to secular culture's unrelenting efforts to define human beings by their sexual activity.[9] Between 1979 and 1984, he delivered a series of addresses that he called, "an *ample commentary* on the doctrine contained in the Encyclical *Humanae Vitae*."[10] These addresses have come to be known as the theology of the body, or as John Paul called it, the *Catechesis on Human Love*, and they are helpful for gaining an understanding of the positive teaching that underlies the Church's prohibitions against contraception, abortion, divorce, and all offenses against the natural human family.

The starting point for the *Catechesis on Human Love* is God's plan for human love and sexuality "in the beginning," as described in the first chapters of the Book of

Genesis. He explains that God, by creating human beings in his image, has made the invisible visible, the intangible tangible. We are made to show forth divine love.

In this way, our bodies may be understood as living metaphors of God's nature—but more than metaphors, because the Son, in becoming human, took on a body like ours and, at the Last Supper, gave his disciples a new commandment: "Love one another; even as I have loved you" (Jn 13:34 RSV). As the Second Vatican Council tells us, Jesus Christ, "by the revelation of the mystery of the Father and His love, fully reveals man to man himself and makes his supreme calling clear" (*Gaudium et Spes* § 22).

And what is our calling? Look again to Jesus' words in his Last Supper discourse. After he gave the love commandment, he prayed to the Father, "that they may all be one . . . as we are one" (Jn 17:21–22). With that prayer, our Lord "opened up vistas closed to human reason, for He implied a certain likeness between the union of the divine persons, and the unity of God's sons in truth and charity. This likeness reveals that man, who is the only creature on earth which God willed for itself, cannot fully find himself except through a sincere gift of himself."[11]

The union of the divine persons is through the love of the Holy Spirit, which is, in its personal essence, Gift. Through this same Holy Spirit love, which dwells in us through our Baptism, we attain the full stature of the divine image imprinted in our nature—filling in the lines of it, if you will—when we give ourselves to God. Our gift to God is that of our entire personhood and—since it is body and soul together that makes the human person—that means it is necessarily an *embodied* gift.

Once we recognize the divine origin and destiny of our bodies, it becomes clear that our actions as they relate to God and to other human beings have meaning far beyond the superficial. When we use our bodies as God has instructed us, especially when we participate in the sacraments, we are revealing a hidden mystery—bringing to earth a bit of heaven.

We see this in Baptism, where, in being washed with water—the means we normally use to cleanse our bodies and make us feel new—the one baptized becomes cleansed in his or her soul, formed into a new creation. We also see it in Communion, where God uses the most mundane physical processes of eating and drinking to bring forth a transcendental encounter, giving us his very self—body, blood, soul, and divinity. We experience it when we enter a confessional and confess our sins to a priest—recognizing when we hear the words, "I absolve you" that, while the voice is the priest's, the true speaker is Christ.

And we witness the hidden mystery of God revealed in a unique way through the shared life of spouses united in the sacrament of Holy Matrimony—a life that includes the gift of their bodies not only through what the Church properly calls the "marital act" and openness to the children that may arise from it but also through an entire life together. Only understood in this context—as the act of a whole person making a "sincere gift of self" to another person in Christ—can sexual intercourse be seen in its proper importance, without making it into a god or denigrating it as though it were inherently godless.

◆ ◆ ◆

Jesus compared heaven to a wedding feast (Mt 22), and John wrote in the book of Revelation that we would all celebrate a wedding in heaven: the marriage of the Church to Jesus (Rv 19:7–9). If you are called to unite yourself in a lifelong gift of love to a spouse, doing so will be, in a very real sense, practice for eternal life in the vision of God and in communion with all the saints.

One of the most beautiful and mysterious things about marriage is that people get so excited about weddings even when they're not terribly religious. Why is that? I mean, when you go to a wedding reception, why are people so exhilarated if all they're celebrating is the fact that John and Judy can finally have socially sanctioned sex whenever they want? Why do people cry at weddings if they're only relieved that Liz can finally have a shot at motherhood before her biological clock runs out?

I think that, on some level, even if they don't fully understand it, people at weddings know that they are witnessing something greater than two people uttering timeworn phrases of fidelity. They know that even if John and Judy have been living together and already have a child, something changes once they're married. They're no longer mere individuals but a couple, with the deepest, strongest commitment two people can have.

Now, if a couple who aren't even religious can feel somehow strengthened by the force of vows made before friends and family, imagine the force the marital commitment takes when made before the eyes of God. A man and woman's commitment to love, honor, and cherish each other as long as they both shall live takes on new meaning and power when they both long with all their hearts for eternal life with God. The gift of self that they give to each other becomes a gift to the Lord.

God rewards the married couple with the gift of being able to participate in his act of creation. This is expressed most supremely in the gift of cooperating with God in procreating children and bringing them into the household of faith. But it is also expressed in a wider sense, in all the love that flourishes between the man and the woman, for as St. Maximilian Kolbe said, "Only love is creative."[12] When a husband and a wife put their hearts, minds, spirits, and bodies together freely, faithfully, totally, and fruitfully, their mutual gift brings forth a spiritual abundance that makes the world a far richer place.[13]

6

GAINING SELF-CONTROL
WITHOUT LOSING YOUR MIND

I once saw a comedy skit in which a man approached a woman at a bar and began a dialogue that went something like this:

> Man: Hi, my name's Joe. Do you come here often?
>
> Woman: No.
>
> Man: Can I buy you a drink?
>
> Woman: No.
>
> Man: Here's my phone number. Can I have yours?
>
> Woman: No.
>
> Man: OK. Well, I'd better be moving on.
>
> Woman: It's been nice "No"-ing you.

When I first made the decision, as a new (not yet Catholic) Christian, to pursue chastity, I thought chastity was simply abstinence—just saying "no."

Is it any surprise, then, that I had a hard time staying chaste? Pursuing something that is purely negative doesn't even make sense; it's like trying not to think of a purple cow.

It wasn't long before I became bitter and resentful about having to forgo my old habits of dress and behavior—habits that, even if ultimately unfulfilling, had at least brought me temporary affirmation and pleasure. On the outside, I was trying to be a happy-clappy Christian, but on the inside, I was wagging my finger at the Almighty: "OK, God, I'm doing this for you, and you'd better appreciate it!"

But I quickly discovered that I couldn't stay chaste if I thought that way. Having emerged from a vicious cycle of brief affairs and painful breakups, I found myself in another vicious cycle: Sin. Repent. Repeat.

Being able to repent at all was a grace, and I was thankful for it. Just the same, it was terribly frustrating to find myself continuing to make the same mistakes, with few signs of improvement.

What broke me out of that cycle was when my friend Dennis, who was then a seminarian (he has since been ordained), gave me a copy of a book on Catholic sexual teaching. It was very, very basic, not a work of great literature by any means. But even watered down, the Gospel truth retains its power to heal. Reading that book was the first time I learned what the Church has always believed about chastity—namely, that chastity is not a negative. Chastity is a virtue, and virtues are never negative. Virtues are always positive. Virtues *enable* us to do things, aided by grace, that we would be unable to accomplish with our own power.

What, then, does chastity enable us to do? The best definition I have heard comes from my friend Paraic Maher:

"Chastity is the virtue that enables us to love fully and completely in every relationship, in the manner that is appropriate to the relationship."

God has designed our bodies in such a way that sex is appropriate only to the married relationship. So, married chastity includes what the Church calls the marital act, but it also includes fidelity and the complete gift of self.

In this way, just as the married relationship is so much more than the marital act, chastity reveals itself to be so much more than refraining from sexual contact. It becomes the virtue that orders earthly loves to the love of God. For each of those whom divine providence places in your life—friends, family, the stranger on the street—you ask yourself, how can I love God through loving this person? As you do, you begin to discover how, throughout your life, God too has been loving *you* through other people.

Learning that was the key to healing for me. I had always thought that if only I could find someone to love me, I would finally be happy and able to love.

That is one reason you shouldn't believe everything you hear in fairy tales. Some of the advice given in fairy tales is just plain wrong. I'm thinking of that line from the film version of *The Wizard of Oz*, where the Wizard, after giving the Tin Man his heart, says, "A heart is not judged by how *much you* love; but by how *much you are loved* by others."

Those words have an inspiring sound when they are voiced in the film. But they are a lie.

The world may judge us by how much we are loved by others. But God judges us by how much we love. More than that, he created us so that the more we love, the more we become who we were created to be. We find our true identity, our true individuality, when we love.

I learned, through discovering chastity, that the greatest tragedy is not that of being unloved. The greatest tragedy is not loving.

◆ ◆ ◆

If you are called to marriage, chastity involves seeing your sexual nature as part of a three-way relationship—and no, that isn't what it sounds like. The relationship is between you, your spouse—or, if you're not yet married, your future spouse—and God. That means if you have sexual intercourse without one corner of that triangle in place—with someone not your spouse, or with your spouse but without faith in God—the act becomes disconnected from its purpose.

In my own experience—and I know I am not alone—the disconnected feeling that results from sexual intercourse outside of marriage can be emotionally disastrous. The illusion of union masks a profound isolation; a pleasure that seems shared is in truth solitary. You are projecting your own hopes and dreams onto your partner—and setting yourself up for heartbreak.

Not only is such disconnectedness painful, but it is also damaging, leading to what writer John Zmirak has called a sort of spiritual bulimia.[1] In attempting to escape loneliness, people who have sexual intercourse outside of marriage, or who fail to place God at the center of their married life, accept a sexual act devoid of spiritual nourishment. Such nourishment is present only within a marital act that is truly *marital*: the sexual union of a man and a woman who have permanently sealed their love to one another within the bond effected by the Holy Spirit through the Sacrament of Matrimony.

John Paul II, in his *Catechesis on Human Love*, speaks of the marital act as an expression of the "language of the body." What spouses speak in their matrimonial vows—promising a free, faithful, total, and fruitful gift of self to one another[2]—they also speak with their bodies when they engage in sexual union. If, in their marital act, husband and wife are not giving themselves to one another freely, faithfully, totally, and fruitfully, then they are telling lies with their bodies—for their bodies are contradicting the promises they made before God.[3]

Interestingly, John Paul II does not say that, if a man and a woman are married neither to one another nor to anyone else, they are telling lies with their body if they engage in sexual intercourse. Why is that? I think it is because, in order for there to be a lie, there has to be speech; for there to be speech, there has to be language; for there to be language, there has to be meaning; for there to be meaning, there has to be truth; and for there to be truth, there has to be love. There can therefore be no "language of the body" in the manner that John Paul means outside of wedding vows—only empty babbling, devoid of grammar or syntax. Remember St. Paul's great declaration at the opening of his great hymn to Christian love: "If I speak in the tongues of men and of angels, but have not love, I am a noisy gong or a clanging cymbal" (1 Cor 13:1 RSV).

With those words, the Holy Spirit teaches us that true language is possible only where there is divine love, for the purpose of language is *communion*. In this light, sexual intercourse between a man and a woman does not even rise to the level of language; it is barely even a human act, for it has no meaning, no truth, and no real love.

I believe that is why St. Ambrose, one of the great Church Fathers and the spiritual father of St. Augustine, refused to call the kiss by which Judas betrayed Jesus a real kiss; he called it rather a "bestial conjunction of the lips."[4] A true kiss can only be one that passes on the peace of Christ:

> A kiss is the sign of love. . . . So the Pharisee
> had no kiss, except perhaps the kiss of the traitor
> Judas. But Judas had no kiss either; and that was
> why, when he wanted to show the Jews the kiss
> he had promised them as the sign of betrayal, the
> Lord said to him, "Judas, betrayest thou the Son

of Man with a kiss?" He meant, do you offer a
kiss when you know not the mystery of the kiss?
It is not the kiss of the lips which is required,
but the kiss of heart and mind [soul]. . . . A kiss
conveys the force of love, and where there is no
love, no faith, no affection, what sweetness can
there be in kisses?[5]

Nicolas Perella notes that Augustine too "regards the
kiss of Judas as the prototype of a lack of correspondence
between the lips and the heart, hence of treachery. . . . The
traitor Judas kissed Christ with his mouth, but in his heart
he was betraying him."[6]

The heart is "our hidden center, beyond the grasp of
our reason and of others," as the *Catechism* puts it; it is "the
place of truth, where we choose life or death. It is the place
of encounter, because as image of God we live in relation:
it is the place of covenant" (*CCC* 2563). If our lips (that is,
our self-expression) are to sincerely correspond to our heart,
our kiss—whether it be of friendship, familial affection, or
spousal love—needs to express God's covenantal love. In
other words, the only kind of self-expression that is true to
our identity as the image of God is an expression of *self-gift*.

When our actions correspond to the divine truth
imprinted in us by virtue of our creation, we experience
the joy and freedom of *integrity*, in which our body, as much
as is possible in this life, works *with* the goodness present
in our soul, instead of against it. Pope Francis speaks of this
integrity in his encyclical *Lumen Fidei* ("The Light of Faith"),
writing that love grounded in truth "unifies all the elements
of our person and becomes a new light pointing the way to
a great and fulfilled life."[7] What is more,

[once] we discover the full light of Christ's love,
we realize that each of the loves in our own lives
had always contained a ray of that light, and we
understand its ultimate destination. That fact

that our human loves contain that ray of light
also helps us to see how all love is meant to share
in the complete self-gift of the Son of God for our
sake. In this circular movement, the light of faith
illumines all our human relationships, which can
then be lived in union with the gentle love of
Christ.[8]

◆ ◆ ◆

Chastity, then, isn't only for the unmarried. It's a lifelong
discipline. Within marriage, it enables us to experience the
fullness of spousal union. But that's not a message you're
going to hear in most of the entertainment media—and
it's certainly not the one that many teenagers are getting
in school. In a classroom culture that discourages public
expressions of faith, teenagers are instead taught—in sex-ed
curricula developed by organizations such as Planned Parenthood—that hormones are destiny.

For decades, Planned Parenthood and its allies have
been waging a campaign against efforts to promote chastity, because they believe it is cruel to expect youths to
overcome their urges. Instead, they treat teens as though
they are automatons, unable to make moral decisions for
themselves.

In this bizarre alternate universe—which, sadly, has
become reality for many of today's youth—good and evil
themselves are redefined. No longer is it bad to allow oneself to use and be used sexually. The only sin is failing to
"protect" oneself by using a condom or another form of
contraception.

Children learn what they see in grown-ups' behavior,
and many adults are only too glad to abdicate moral responsibility. Once faith lost its place in modern culture—as it
did during the mid-1960s, when the cover of a top-selling

magazine asked, "Is God Dead?"—the concept of chastity became worse than irrelevant. It was unfathomable.

But chastity didn't disappear. As with the early Christians in the Roman catacombs, it went underground. Today, as the fruits of the sexual revolution prove to be loneliness, divorce, and disease, not only has chastity resurfaced, it's the new counterculture. Chastity is so out, it's in.

Living chastely is a bold challenge to modern culture, because it proves that people are not automatons but human beings with free will. Only individuals who are truly free can place themselves under a vow, whether the vow is one of marriage or of religious life. Slaves do not have such power.

To vow or consecrate himself or herself, and live by that vow or consecration, is the most radical act of freedom that a human being can make. Contemplating that fact, it becomes clear why governments, when they turn atheistic and totalitarian, begin to aggressively seek to subvert or destroy the institutions where chastity is most prized: marriage and consecrated religious life. Those institutions, by their very existence, give the lie to philosophies that would set up man himself as a god, for they reveal instead the image of God in man—in the free will that enables man to find his perfection "in seeking and loving what is true and good."[9]

◆ ◆ ◆

The symbol of early Christians was a fish—perhaps inspired in part by Jesus saying he would make his disciples "fishers of men" (Mt 4:19 RSV)—and, as with the salmon swimming upstream, we're charged to go against the flow. I battle the destructive currents of secular culture, because it's the only right way to use the abundant life that has been given to me. As G. K. Chesterton wrote, "A dead thing can go with the stream, but only a living thing can go against it."[10]

Chesterton is beloved by Christians as a vocal defender of truth against efforts by government and individuals to redefine morality. Less known is that, even as he criticized the harmful ideas of his contemporaries, he saved his strongest criticism for himself. This was no false humility; he knew he was a gifted writer. (See, for example, his two-sentence introduction to his book on George Bernard Shaw: "Most people say that they agree with Bernard Shaw or that they do not understand him. I am the only person who understands him, and I do not agree with him."[11]) Yet he also had a clear-eyed understanding of his own sinfulness and his need for God.

There is a popular anecdote about Chesterton—perhaps only a legend but one that reveals a deeper truth about how the great writer saw himself. The story goes that a London newspaper, after publishing a series of essays titled "What's Wrong with the World?" received this letter:

> Dear Sir: Regarding your article "What's Wrong with the World?" I am. Yours truly,
>
> G. K. Chesterton

In a similar vein, Chesterton said (in a quote that is a favorite of Pope Emeritus Benedict XVI), "Angels can fly because they can take themselves lightly."[12] It was because he was serious about his faith that he could laugh at himself.

I take heart from Chesterton's example of humility, because I need to remember my own failings if I am to see beyond present difficulties. For the hardest thing about being chaste is not, as modern culture would have it, keeping your libido in check. Any person of sound mind and body can say "no" to genital activity if he tries hard enough. No, the hardest thing about being chaste is saying "*yes*"—to effectively say with lips and heart together, "*Yes*, I believe God made me in his image! *Yes*, I believe Jesus shows me how to live out my identity as a beloved child of the Father,

by giving and receiving chaste love! *Yes,* I believe the Holy
Spirit will enable me to make an ever-more-beautiful gift
of myself to God and neighbor, even in the midst of suffering. . . ."

I believe I need to stop and take a breath! Those are
strong words, and they present a challenge to me even as I
write them. Can I honestly say I feel such faith? But that is
the wrong question to ask. For, as I wrote in *My Peace I Give
You,* faith is not a feeling—and thank God for that! Rather,
faith is a *lived reality:*

> At every Sunday Mass, Catholics recite the Creed:
> "I believe in one God . . ." In the original Greek,
> the word *eis,* translated as "in," literally bears
> a meaning closer to "into." What we are really
> saying is not merely that we make the intellec-
> tual choice to believe, but that we believe with
> *understanding*—an understanding that actually
> draws us into union with God, the object of our
> faith. Faith, on this account, is more than mere
> acknowledgment of the Creator. It is a dynamic
> principle that draws us forward to God, carried
> by grace, whether we feel its operations or not.
>
> There have been moments in my life when
> I have been blessed with the consoling feeling of
> the Lord's presence. It is an unspeakably beau-
> tiful sensation, and I long to have it again. But I
> have come to realize that, in the long run, there
> is something even more consoling than momen-
> tarily sensing the nearness of God. It is the sure
> knowledge that regardless of how I may feel at
> any given moment (for feelings, as we all know,
> can come and go), my heart is united to God
> because *I believe.*[13]

7

BECOMING A SINGULAR
SENSATION

A New York City university recently offered continuing-education students a course on "Living Single."

"Now, more than at any other time, the single lifestyle is viewed as a viable, desirable choice for men and women," read the course description. "Whether they find themselves single again, or single still, many adults are not completely comfortable flying solo—or confident in their ability to do it successfully. Topics include: viewing the contemporary world; relating to couples; the dating scene, how to be part of it (or not); and battling the blues that sometimes arise. Enrich your life with resources on what to read, pursue, reflect on, and talk about to gain confidence with single living." As a final note, the description added, "No grades are given for this course." Phew! What a relief. After getting your certificate in "Living Single," wouldn't you hate to have to confess to a new love interest that you got a C minus in "viewing the contemporary world"?

I don't want to be unfair. Since the divorce rate spiked in the early 1970s, society has become more atomized than ever before, leading the unmarried and unattached to feel increasingly isolated. So I can understand why some people might be attracted to a course that claims to help singles face the unique challenges of their state of life. But honestly, as I read that course description touting, "the single lifestyle," it all seems to boil down to a single word: lack.

The paradigm for modern singlehood is yin without yang. To avoid "pronoun trouble," I'll speak of it from my own experience as a woman, but this by no means applies to ladies only; you can switch the references to the sexes anywhere in this chapter and the point will be the same: the modern single woman's goal is to relate to love interests from a single perspective and to have fulfilling relationships with them without ever becoming part of anything larger than herself. As my parents' generation would have said, she is on her own trip.

For the unmarried woman who harbors the least bit of longing for something deeper, this modern-singlehood rut ultimately devolves into the familiar merry-go-round of pursuing, or being pursued, by almost-but-not-quite-right love interests, revolving around the hope that the ever-distant Mr. Right will come along one day and stop the music. During the years when I believed I was called to marriage, I found that whole mind-set terribly stifling, and I think most other singles do too—they certainly complain about it enough. Yet, most seem helpless to find an alternative.

The truth is that there is another way, but few singles want to think about it. No one wants to get off of a merry-go-round while it's still spinning. Sometimes, however, that is the only way to avoid a ride to nowhere.

A woman who has the courage to step out into the unknown, risking temporary loneliness for a shot at lasting joy, is more than a "single." She is *singular*. Instead of defining herself by what she lacks—a relationship with a man—she defines herself by what she has: a relationship with God.

A single woman bases her actions on how they will or won't affect her single, lacking state. She goes to parties based on whether or not there will be new men to meet; if there won't then the food and drink had better be first rate. She chooses female friends who likewise define themselves as single and lacking, thus reinforcing her own cynicism.

But a singular woman bases her actions on how they will enable her to be the person she believes God wants her to be. She trusts that God has a plan for her and that no matter what suffering may come, she will find joy if she seeks nothing but God's will, making the best use of the gifts she has been given. She'll still enjoy parties and meeting people—but as ends in and of themselves, not just as a means of finding a man.

A single woman, in seeking a husband, feels the need to act in a coy, sly, or deceptive manner—even if she normally would never think of intentionally misleading someone. Somehow, within the parameters of a budding relationship, to be cagey with a man doesn't seem wrong to her. Likewise, she accepts a level of superficiality from a man she's dating that she wouldn't tolerate from her friends. She's not stupid—she just loses perspective when facing the possibility of a relationship. Her brain compartmentalizes dating into its own relative morality: "all's fair in love and war."

A singular woman behaves with an honesty and lack of guile that will appear arresting to the love interest who expects a superficial relationship—as well it should. With her words and actions, she is speaking a deeper language, one that can be understood only by the kind of man for whom she longs—one of integrity. Such a man will understand that the singular woman's straightforwardness and absence of pretense is rooted in deep respect for him as a fellow child of God. For example, Miss Singular is not going to suggest to her love interest that he faces competition for her if that is not currently the case. She expects him to be equally truthful in return.

Perhaps the most noticeable difference between a single woman and a singular woman is that of gratitude. Because the single woman defines herself by her lack, she is plagued with a sense of sadness and resentment at what she doesn't have. When positive things happen in her life, she may be thankful, but she may just as well respond with a sense of entitlement—"At last, I'm getting what everyone else has."

The singular woman not only expresses more gratitude than the single woman but also expresses it for different things. She's grateful not only for things she receives but also for the opportunities she has to give. She knows in her heart the spirit of G. K. Chesterton's words: "The world will never starve for want of wonders; but only for want of wonder."[1]

Being single places you in a mental cage where your value is measured by what you do, whether good or bad: how well you are able to attract men, acquire friends, make money, say witty things, and put forth other social commodities. Ultimately, your capacity in these areas is finite; you can do only so much before you've exhausted your resources. The world may say you can never be too rich or too thin, but all it takes is a look at celebrities' love lives to see that wealth and slenderness don't guarantee happiness. (That's not to say I wouldn't be very happy to squeeze into the size 6 silver lamé 1960s minidress I bought for $45 dollars on what turned out to be the only day of my life that I ever weighed under 115 pounds. On second thought, however, it probably wouldn't be well received at the Dominican-run school of theology I now attend.)

To be singular is to embark on a wide excursion of discovery. No more is your identity limited to qualities that can be defined by the check off boxes in an online profile or personal ad. It's no longer what you do, but who you are. Prayerfully, you strive to develop inner qualities, including empathy, patience, humility, and faith in spite of hardship.

Such a transition is not easy, especially when your temptation around an attractive man is to shift back into your single self. There's a comforting familiarity in interacting with others on a superficial level and knowing that they will interact with you in the same way. But I can tell you from experience that the more you develop a singular identity, the more confident you will become around men and in every area of your life, because you will be comfortable in your own skin.

◆◆◆

When I wrote the above words for the original version of this chapter, in 2005, I was only just beginning to gain peace after struggling to overcome the temptation to seek love through sexual attention from men. I went on in the chapter to share some personal memories. It is difficult for me to read them now, but I am sharing them with you because many people have told me they were helped by them:

> I spent many years of my life being single. I have nothing to show for it except the ability to toss my hair fetchingly and a mental catalog of a thousand banal things to say to fill the awkward, unbearably lonely moments between having sex and putting my clothes back on. You never see those moments in TV or movies, because they strike to the core of the black hole that casual sex can never fill.

Now that I'm singular, I understand why the popular culture tries so relentlessly to define single women as superficial and libidinous singles rather than deep singulars who value marriage enough to hold out for it. To be singular is to understand the meaning of chastity, and chastity by its very nature goes against the popular culture's beliefs regarding sex and choice.

The culture tells unmarried women that it is perfectly normal and acceptable to act on our sexual desires—all the way. We only have to take the right precautions—physical ones, such as using a condom—and we are "safe." What is abnormal, and even destructive, in the eyes of the culture, is to resist such desires, especially if we are doing so for moral reasons. The concept of deferring pleasure makes no sense in a consumer society where we are told we must take something when it's offered or risk it going off the market. We're told that even though men come and go like buses, the next one may not be such a good ride.

In light of such social prejudices, a singular woman is a revolutionary. Think about it: all it takes is one unmarried woman to live a dynamic, well-rounded, and happy life while avoiding premarital sex, and the culture's image of the drab spinster crumbles like a house of cards. That's why being singular is so exciting. It's an act of open rebellion—liberating you from an oppressive culture.

◆ ◆ ◆

If there is one quality that marks our culture's conception of singlehood, it is hunger. A single woman who's up front about her desire to meet someone is seen as "man hungry." If she's been looking for a while, she's viewed as "sex-starved" or "starved for affection."

The media would have you believe that the hunger of love may be satisfied as simply as the hunger for food. You find that for which you hunger—be it a bagel or a bachelor—indulge yourself, and then go on with your daily life until you get hungry again. But there is, in fact, a fundamental difference between the two desires.

Hunger for food points directly to the object that satisfies it. Despite our individual tastes, this hunger isn't divided into higher and lower forms. Whether we'd rather eat sushi or cottage cheese, the pangs are the same. If we eat enough of anything, we'll experience the feeling of being full.

Hunger for love points *beyond* the object that satisfies it. If a married woman loves her husband, her desire to be loved in return is not fulfilled simply because her husband says he loves her. Nor is it fulfilled only because he treats her kindly or gives her presents. It's not even fulfilled just because, in addition to showing all manner of devotion, he engages in the marital act with her. We all know that a spouse can do all these things and not be in love.

The love between husband and wife, as with all types of love, is fulfilled only when both partners together look beyond externals and discover that something they can't describe binds them together. That something, I believe, is God's own love, and it may truly be called a taste of heaven. It is the food for which we hunger most, even when our desires tell us that a longed-for mate holds the promise of satisfaction.

When Jesus saw the Samaritan woman approach the well where he was sitting and told her he could give her "living water" (Jn 4:10 RSV), the woman thought at first that he was simply offering to quench her physical thirst. I know how she felt. When you're used to being treated according to how useful you are—and treating others the same way—your expectations are lower. You also become less able to give of yourself, because you lose sight of the qualities that are truly valuable—the "fruit of the Spirit" (Gal 5:22 RSV).

So, the Samaritan woman, thinking literally, said, "Sir, give me this water" (Jn 4:15 RSV). Jesus' response came out of left field: "Go, call your husband, and come here" (Jn 4:16 RSV). When the woman answered that she had no husband, Jesus said to her, "You are right in saying, 'I have no husband'; for you have had five husbands, and he whom you now have is not your husband; this you said truly" (Jn 4:17–18 RSV).

Notice what Jesus was doing in speaking that way to the woman—and what he wasn't doing. He shifted the topic from the woman's physical needs to what was really troubling her—her spiritual needs. She hungered for something that five husbands and a live-in boyfriend could not fulfill. Yet, Jesus didn't pass judgment on the woman. Instead, he held a mirror to her conscience. She listened to him from then on with an open heart. The revelation he gave led her to run to the nearby city, telling the people, "Come, see a man who told me all that I ever did. Can this be the Christ?" (Jn 4:29 RSV).

We know that the woman's desire to bring people to Jesus was not because he literally told her all she had ever done. What he did was offer her the truth that enabled her to see clearly, for the first time, her life and her long-ings. What she saw cut her to the heart. She was able to understand the truth Jesus gave, because she herself was truthful—admitting to Jesus that something was missing from her life.

If you want to receive the love for which you hunger, the first step is to admit to yourself that you have that hunger, with everything it entails: weakness, vulnerability, and the feeling of an empty space inside. To tell yourself simply, "I'll be happy once I have someone to love," is to deny the depth and seriousness of your longing. It turns the hunger into a superficial desire for flesh and blood when what we really want is someone to share divine love with us, to be for us "God with skin on."

Psalm 107 tells what God has in store for those who have this spiritual hunger:

> He turns a desert into pools of water, a parched
> land into springs of water. And there he lets the
> hungry dwell, and they establish a city to live in.
> (vv. 35–36 RSV)

What does this tell us? You could say that it means God will
feed us. But there's a deeper message: to live in the city of
God, *you must be hungry*. It doesn't say, "God takes the satisfied people and sets them up so they can stay satisfied."
It says, "There he lets the hungry dwell."

The psalmist is referring to the same hunger felt by the
Samaritan woman who asked Jesus for the living water, and
the same longing that Jesus speaks of in the Sermon on the
Mount, when he blesses "those who hunger and thirst for
righteousness" (Mt 5:6 RSV). By hungering and thirsting
after righteousness, Jesus means not merely longing to do
right but longing to exist in a right state with God. It's the
deep-seated desire to align your heart with his so that, in
your love for him and for your neighbor, you may become
like him.

When you are hungry, really hungry, it's hard to think
about anything else. Likewise, hungering for righteousness
means not being able to rest until your hunger is satisfied,
as with St. Augustine when he cried out to God, "Our
hearts are restless till we find rest in you."[2]

A reporter once asked one of Hollywood's greatest
beauties her secret to keeping her weight down. Her answer
was not what the dieters of this world had been waiting for.
She said she ate small portions, never allowing herself to
get full. Always, she said, she left the dining table a little
hungry. When I first read that story, I thought sarcastically,
Well, good for her. I was and am determined to leave the
dining table full even if it means loading up on broccoli. But
when it comes to spiritual hunger, we too should always
leave the table having been fed and yet still with room for

more. Our citizenship is in heaven. We are not meant to be fully satisfied on this earth.

Thankfully, there are things we can do in this life to draw closer to the spiritual food that will fill us in the world to come. We can even taste it—especially at Mass, where we receive "the bread of life from the table both of God's word and of Christ's body."[3]

Here's an exercise you can practice today. Whenever you feel hungry or thirsty, before you fulfill that need, get in touch with it and try to grasp—just for a moment—how dependent you are on God for everything in your life. Make friends with that sense of longing, and it will change your whole way of life.

Hunger—true spiritual hunger—is a gift. Cherish it.

8

THE AGONY AND THE ECSTASY

Walking to a Manhattan train station after work one night during my early days of chastity, I passed a bus shelter ad touting a British television comedy with the slogan "Love, lust, and everything in between."

Something about the slogan seemed not right. I pondered it a moment, and the answer hit me: there is *nothing* "in between" love and lust. I don't mean that the two are the same. I mean that they're not on the same continuum. Try to substitute those nouns with others equally disparate and you'll see what I mean. "Hatred, head colds, and everything in between." "Irony, iron deficiency, and everything in between." It's ludicrous.

Admittedly, it is possible to confuse lust with love—just as it's possible to think that the whole world is against you when you've really only forgotten to have your first cup of coffee. Recall the exchange in Charles Dickens's short story *A Christmas Carol* between Marley's ghost and an incredulous Scrooge:

"Why do you doubt your senses?"

"Because," said Scrooge, "a little thing affects them. A slight disorder of the stomach makes them cheats. You may be an undigested bit of beef, a blot of mustard, a crumb of cheese, a fragment of an underdone potato. There's more of gravy than of grave about you, whatever you are!"[1]

It's the same thing with our sexual appetite as it is with our appetite for food. An attractive face may awaken the undigested ghost of an old flame. But the feeling isn't comparable to love—neither in kind nor in degree.

Yet our culture—not just the media but society in general—relentlessly puts forth the idea that lust is a way station on the road to love. Make that more than a way station: it's more like an indefinite layover. This misguided, hedonistic philosophy harms everyone, though my own experience leads me to believe it is particularly damaging to women. To be sure, men and women alike are created by God with the intention that Christ be formed in them (see Gal 4:19) and that they bear his love to others. But women are literally built to bear new life within themselves.

So much social pressure is laid upon women to keep them from asserting that their interior experience of their sexuality is different from that of men. But as long as fertility remains such a fact of womanhood that it cannot be constrained save by chemicals, surgery, or other manipulations, the truth cannot be suppressed. This I can tell you from my lived experience: women are vessels, and they seek to be filled. For that reason, sexual intercourse will always leave them feeling empty unless they are certain that they are loved.

◆ ◆ ◆

At the time of the so-called sexual revolution during the 1960s, media figures such as *Cosmopolitan* magazine editor Helen Gurley Brown tried to sell women on the bizarre fantasy that they could "have sex like a man." Their thinking, as I understand it, was that women's happiness was being impeded by the cultural belief that commitment-free sexual intercourse was emotionally harmful to them. If only society permitted them to engage in encounters with whomever they chose, without the burden of social stigma or religion-induced guilt, women would be able to maximize their sexual satisfaction while remaining blissfully dissociated from their emotions—just as men do! (Just as *psychopathic* men do, that is. No man could actually live the Helen Gurley Brown dream without suffering lasting emotional dysfunction.)

Although the expression, "having sex like a man" has gone out of fashion (women aren't encouraged to do *anything* "like a man" anymore), popular culture still holds up for our example celebrities who claim to have perfected the art of engaging in no-strings-attached sexual encounters. But the idea that attempting to detach body from soul (or actions from personal identity) is healthy has never been the teaching of the Catholic Church. Against a culture that strives to dissociate flesh from spirit, the Church insists that body and soul are a unity: "The human body shares in the dignity of 'the image of God': it is a human body precisely because it is animated by a spiritual soul, and it is the whole human person that is intended to become, in the body of Christ, a temple of the Spirit" (*CCC* 364).

As I write in *My Peace I Give You*, through the way we know and experience things, we can easily see that the human body is more than a mere mechanism:

> In each person, intellect, understanding, and will do not exist in a vacuum; they are embodied. When I am standing in a crowded subway

car and someone steps on my toe, I know that
it is *my* toe that was stepped on, because I feel
the pain. Somebody didn't just step on my toe;
they stepped on *me*. At the same time, I am conscious that the person who stepped on my toe
is someone who is *not* me. If my soul only happened to be connected with my body, and was
not united with it in the deepest, innermost way,
how would I know I was separate from anyone
else? How would I feel an attack on my body as
being an attack on myself? It is my basic human
experience of the reality of my own unity of body
and soul that enables me to function as a human
being and have relationships with others.[2]

Because of the unity of body and soul, it's important to
realize that, if you felt hurt after crossing physical boundaries with someone who proved himself or herself unworthy
of your affection, the pain was not because—as so many in
our sex-obsessed culture would claim—you were doing it
wrong. It's because you were doing it *right*. It's the situation
itself—seeking physical excitement for its own sake, outside
the love and security of a marital relationship—that was
wrong. When a man and a woman unite their bodies in
sexual union, the natural outcome, for both of them, is that
they experience themselves as vulnerable, not just physically, but emotionally as well. People of course can and do
try to suppress or numb that feeling, but even the fact that
such suppression takes effort shows that the act of sex feels
bonding by its very nature.

◆ ◆ ◆

What's behind the cultural determination to make dissociation fashionable? In a word: cynicism. Entertainment producers and media editors, thirsting to attract advertisers,
promote the fantasy of dissociation, all the while knowing

in their tin hearts that sexual objectification doesn't really make people happy. That's why they continually put graphic sexual images in our faces and obscene language in our ears. It's their way of creating an empty hole of dissatisfaction that they can then use to fool us into buying products that distract us from seeking "treasures in heaven, where neither moth nor decay destroys, nor thieves break in and steal" (Mt 6:20).

One holy woman of the twentieth century who knew firsthand the vacuousness behind the culture's glamorization of sexual sin was Dorothy Day, the cofounder of the Catholic Worker movement. Dorothy, whose cause has been introduced for canonization, is often called an "American Mother Teresa" for her work helping the poor and suffering. However, as she confessed in her memoir *The Long Loneliness*, her lifestyle during her late teens and twenties was far from saintly.

Kicked out of her home as a teenager after her father objected to her taking a newspaper job (a sportswriter himself, he thought a newspaper was "no place for a woman"), Dorothy became a radical political activist who drank, smoked, and had affairs. At twenty-two, in a choice she would deeply regret, she aborted her child in a desperate (and unsuccessful) attempt to keep her boyfriend from leaving. Her decision eight years later to enter the Church at age thirty cost her the great love of her life, an atheist who was the father of her only surviving child.

Reflecting upon her conversion, Dorothy recalled how her radical friends claimed she entered the Church because she was "tired of sex, satiated, disillusioned."[3] The real reason was beyond their comprehension: "It was because through a whole love, both physical and spiritual, I came to know God."

Dorothy's experience echoed what Christians have endured through the ages, especially those who once ran with the crowd: daily life for those who dare to resist secular culture's temptations is filled with reminders that they are in this world but not of it. The strain of constant conflict with an unsympathetic culture was especially familiar to the faithful during the early years of the Church. St. Paul described it in his letter to the Philippians: "For to you has been granted, for the sake of Christ, not only to believe in him but also to suffer for him. Yours is the same struggle as you saw in me and now hear about me" (Phil 1:29–30).

But it's more than a mere struggle. The word Paul uses that the New American Bible translates as "struggle" is really *agon*—Greek for "agony." The word *agon* appears several times in Paul's letters. Each time, it refers to an earthly conflict that requires faith to overcome—an ongoing battle that we will fight as long as we are in this mortal coil. "Agony" doesn't mean sudden, sharp bursts of pain but rather a long, drawn-out ordeal. That makes it a fitting term to describe the ongoing battle faced by those who strive to align their own wills with God's will for them.

The most challenging part of chastity isn't overcoming temptations. It's gaining the spiritual resources to joyfully face day-to-day life as a cultural outsider. It's a conflict between pleasing men and pleasing God. This is the "good fight" of faith that Paul describes in both 1 Timothy 6:12 and 2 Timothy 4:7—and it's no coincidence that the word he uses for "fight" in both cases is *agon*.

There must be a reason why people, in the face of loneliness and isolation, are willing to forgo physical pleasures in hope of spiritual joys. For me (and here I'm thinking back to when I still believed I was called to marriage), it's because I became convinced that, contrary to what our culture claims, my readiness to engage in physical intimacy outside of marriage was not a healthy way to be. Just permitting myself to make a man into the object of my sexual fantasies altered me to the point that I was not equipped to sustain a marriage. People don't marry a mental construct of a sex object; they marry another *person*. As long as I was seeking sex, even if I was really seeking love through sex, I wasn't truly open to the gift of a flesh-and-blood man to love.

Jesus endured the Cross, "for the joy that was set before him" (Heb 12:2 RSV). When I first started pursuing chastity, I could not always see the joy that is set before me. But I knew one thing. Where my old way of life was concerned, there was no joy behind me. There was nothing about my way of life before I became chaste that I could possibly revisit and be truly happy. If joy really existed— and I believed it did; otherwise, I wouldn't be alive—then it had to be ahead.

◆ ◆ ◆

As a newcomer to chastity, undoing the lies of the culture required me to proactively reeducate myself. Secular culture would have me believe, as the writers of a sex-obsessed television show put it, "The most exciting, challenging, and significant relationship of all is the one you have with yourself. And if you can find someone to love the 'you' you love, well, that's just fabulous."[4]

When I heard that, I reflected and realized I've had an exciting, challenging, and significant relationship with myself for more than three decades. It's not hard for me to find someone to love the me I love. What I never imagined before I was chaste was that I could hope to find someone to love the me I *don't* love. My weaknesses, my insecurities, my shortcomings, and all the times I miss the mark.

Through changing the way I perceived myself and the world, looking beyond appearances, I finally began to gain a real understanding of love beyond the glamorous but ultimately vapid Hollywood fantasies. I came to realize that all that time I thought I was romanticizing love in my mind, I was really limiting it. What seemed like cockeyed optimism was actually coarse cynicism.

And so, as I entered into a way of life that the world claimed was madness (and still does), I became, against all odds, hopelessly . . . hopeful. I knew there could be many more nights of walking down lonely streets and being mocked by bus shelter ads. But I came believe that the only real "in between" isn't between lust and love. It's between this world and the kingdom of God. Running the race across that divide, however exhausting, is worth the *agon*.

9

SAYING YES LIKE YOU MEAN IT

Some people who don't really know what chastity means assume it is too simplistic for sophisticated adults—a relic from the era when schoolchildren were given the anti-drug message, "Just say no." The truth is that it's far more nuanced. In the language of chastity, no means yes—and yes means no. I'm not talking about consent but about the issues behind consent. When you say yes or no, what are you really saying yes or no to?

Modern secular culture embraces relativism—the idea that my "truth" is no better than your "truth," and vice versa. But when it comes to sex, the tables are turned. Those whom society calls "tolerant" or "open-minded" see things only in black and white, while the chaste counterculture sees boundless shades of gray.

You can see the contrast in perspectives through the way the popular culture equates chastity with abstinence. In reality, while abstaining from sexual contact may be part of chastity, the chastity concept goes far beyond keeping your clothes on (the subtitle of this book notwithstanding). It's a discipline that engages mind, body, and spirit.

A man or woman can be abstinent and not be chaste; tales of the Desert Fathers (the earliest Christian hermits) bound with accounts of celibates who battled the temptation to engage in sexual fantasies. Likewise, if one is married and treats one's partner with love, respect, and fidelity, one can be chaste and not abstinent. (In fact, save for extraordinary exceptions—think Mary and Joseph— if spouses were to maintain complete sexual abstinence throughout their marriage, they would be acting *against* marital chastity. That is because marital chastity, by its nature, includes sexual intercourse; this is why the Church calls sexual intercourse the "marital act.")

The relativists' idea of sex as being genital-centered may create a neat dividing line, but it ultimately looks upon man as a mere animal whose sexual experience is limited to physical sensations. By contrast, the chaste know that there is more to sex than slobber-slobber-huff-puff-push-push-bang. Likewise, they know that saying yes has far more layers of meaning than simply, "Give me what you know I want."

◆ ◆ ◆

In his letter to the Philippians, Paul wrote, "Work out your own salvation" (Phil 2:12 RSV). When, at thirty-one, I first became aware of Christ's saving power (but had not yet accepted the truth of Catholic faith), I had a *lot* to work out.

I knew that as a new Christian, certain things were expected of me. The gift of faith, which came unexpectedly, required me to strive upward. Although I had yet to understand the nature of chastity, I knew I had to stop allowing myself to use men or be used by them sexually.

And yet . . . there was a nagging voice inside my mind saying that sexual sins were pretty low on God's list of dislikes. Thinking of the popular bumper sticker, "Christians aren't perfect—just forgiven," I decided I would try to avoid premarital sex but with a fallback plan. If I gave into temptation, all I would have to do was ask God for forgiveness. Then, by his own rules, he'd have to let me back onto heaven's waiting list.

What was lacking from my theology was an understanding of the infectious nature of sin. While my conversion had been dramatic—healing me not only of my unbelief but also of the depression that had plagued me since my teen years—I still had the wrong idea about what really happened when I broke a commandment. (Sex outside marriage breaks the sixth commandment, which the tradition of the Church understands as "encompassing the whole of human sexuality" [CCC 2336], calling everyone to purity. If your heart's desire is to hear your intended vow to love and honor you all the days of his or her life, then it breaks the golden rule as well. Think about it.)

Without realizing it, I was treating divine law as though it was arbitrarily imposed from outside—as though I did not have the Most Holy Trinity dwelling within me through my Baptism.[1] It's hard today to recall exactly how I rationalized this. I think my underlying assumption was that the commandments were there merely to protect me from possible earthly repercussions to bad behavior. My self-serving attitude effectively reduced God to a utilitarian, with the commandment against adultery merely a helpful hint to keep me from becoming jaded.

Not until about six months after becoming a Christian did it begin to hit me that my moral compass was off kilter. It happened during a visit to a crowded Manhattan music collectors' fair. I heard a man call my name, turned around, and found myself face-to-face with an ex-lover I had not seen in three years. Looking at George (not his real name), a host of emotions rose up within me—affection, fear, and, most of all, an overpowering sense of shame.

Partly I was ashamed because George's presence brought to mind the sexual sins of my past. But more than that, I was ashamed because this man and I had been engaged in something worse than unchastity. Together we had harmed another person through our shared selfishness and dishonesty. Even when I was an agnostic, I knew our relationship was horribly wrong; the guilt nearly drove me to suicide. It was no wonder that now, as a Christian, the very sight of him made me shudder.

George looked different from the last time I had seen him. He was now thin and drawn, his face bearing deep lines. He informed me that he had been diagnosed with a rare form of cancer. "I'm determined to beat this thing," he said. But there was something about the way he said it that made me realize he wouldn't. Fingering my cross necklace nervously, I asked if he was religious. He told me he wasn't in the least; in fact, he was very cynical about faith. I didn't know how to respond. Trying to remember the words of St. Paul, I sputtered something about mortifying the body (see Rom 8:13). I meant that he should be chaste, but the way it came out, it sounded pretty morbid.

That was the last time I saw George. A year later, I read in a local paper that he'd died of his illness. The thought of him unrepentant on his deathbed haunted me. For the first time, I started to wonder what effect my own sexual sins had on the men with whom I'd sinned. If Christians weren't perfect, just forgiven, then what about the trail of wreckage that *this* forgiven Christian had left in her wake? Worse, what would happen if I continued to presume upon God's mercy for myself while blithely ignoring my sins' toxic fallout?

Even as my sensitivity to sin grew, I had a very hard time getting the chastity message from my heart and mind to the rest of my body. The turning point came two and a half years after my run-in with George, during my first date

with a *New York Post* colleague on whom I'd had a crush
for some months.

I knew right off that Bill wasn't marriage material. He
was a playboy, he didn't share my faith, and he was hung
up on a woman he still called his fiancée even though she'd
gotten cold feet and moved to Australia. So, why was I with
him at all? The answer is the classic excuse, one that, as a
friend of mine puts it, would never hold up in court: "I was
lonely, Your Honor." Once you allow yourself to be defined
by your loneliness, it's a small step to violating your most
deeply held beliefs.

Bill and I were on the couch in his West Village apartment, in the preliminary movements of a clumsy, self-conscious kind of dance I knew well from my pre-Christian
days. The attraction that had long simmered in our newsroom conversations was finally, seemingly inevitably, bub-
bling to the surface. We were about a minute and a half
away from moving to his bed when I suddenly broke free
and stood up.

"I—I haven't done this in a while . . . and I'm feeling
really uncomfortable," I said. That probably would have
been enough, but I had something inside that had to get
out. Before I knew it, I was crying. What had hit me was
that by intending to have sexual intercourse with Bill, I was
disrespecting God. If the Lord intended me to marry (and,
at the time, I believed he did), then my future husband
was somewhere out there. To fool around with a man who
was so clearly not the one whom God, in his divine providence, had chosen for me was to say to my Maker, in effect,
"You've been taking your precious time. Well, I don't have
to wait for you. In fact, I don't even think you're playing
with a full deck. Since you're not giving me what I want,
I'm going to take what I can get. So there, Mr. Omnipotent."

I explained all this to Bill, declaiming dramatically as
I stood on his living room carpet while he sat on his couch
with a quizzical expression on his face. He must have been

shocked, but he politely humored me as I composed myself and made my exit.

I went home still lonely but with a feeling that something had changed. For the first time, I realized that all the times I'd said yes, I'd really said no. Each time I'd said yes to sexual intercourse outside marriage, I had really said no to the friendship of God. More than that, I was denying my sex partner friendship with God by enabling him to act in a way that went against God's will for him.

I say "friendship," because friendship is a two-way street. God is always ready to be our friend, but he can bring us into union with him only if we allow him to be Lord of every aspect of our lives. Jesus told his disciples, "If a man loves me, he will keep my word, and my Father will love him, and we will come to him and make our home with him" (Jn 14:23 RSV). The Holy Spirit can't make his home in you when you shut the door.

If you want to change your life for the better, you must be completely open to experiencing the blessings God has for you. That's why chastity isn't about saying no. It's about saying *yes.*

◆ ◆ ◆

Back when I was in high school, long before I believed, my mother and I lived in a New Jersey suburb where there was a Catholic church called Our Lady of Sorrows. I remember thinking, "What a depressing name for a church! Who would want to go there?" I didn't understand the meaning of Mary's sorrows because I didn't understand the meaning of her *joys.*

Years later, when I began to study the Catholic faith, I discovered a reflection by Fulton J. Sheen about the metaphorical sword that passed through Mary's soul during the each of the traumas that tradition calls her Seven Sorrows. Sheen writes that, with each of the Seven Sorrows, the sword first pierced Jesus' own heart before it pierced that of his Mother: "Nothing enters into her soul that has not first entered into His."[2] The depth of Sheen's insight was beyond my comprehension. I tried but could not understand what difference it made that each of Mary's interior wounds was first experienced by Christ. How could that assuage her pain?

Only after I had been a Catholic for some time did Sheen's meaning begin to dawn on me. Reading about the dogma of the Immaculate Conception, I learned that Mary had the "singular grace and privilege" of being preserved from original sin by virtue of the foreseen merits of Christ, specifically the merits that Christ would win for humanity through his Passion.[3] God could give Mary this grace even though her birth was prior to her Son's historical existence because, although Jesus' human nature became incarnate within time, it was fully united to his divine nature, which is eternal. Therefore, Jesus' human will to redeem humanity by his suffering, by virtue of its union with his divine will, had the power to redeem his own mother from the first moment of her existence.

Learning about how Mary was redeemed led me to think about the implications of the Gospel metaphor of the sword in light of Sheen's reflections. When a sword passes through one heart, and then immediately passes through another heart, the second heart, as it is pierced, comes into contact with the first heart's blood. In the same way, spiritually speaking, if the sword of redemptive suffering that pierced Mary's Immaculate Heart was the same sword that first entered into her Son's Sacred Heart, then her suffering was intimately united with Jesus' blood that was "poured out for many for the forgiveness of sins" (Mt 26:28 RSV). We could even say that Mary's suffering was *suffused* with the grace of Christ—a grace that gave her, even in her deepest pain, the joy of unbroken contact with her Son's divine love.

Now, think back to the Annunciation—the moment when Mary, in answering the angel Gabriel, gave her great yes to God: "Behold, I am the handmaid of the Lord. May it be done to me according to your word" (Lk 1:38). Mary's words carry a decisive finality. She is not just consenting to a temporary intervention of God in her life. It is not as though she intended that the Holy Spirit, having conceived Jesus in her womb, should then leave her so she could do her own thing. Rather, Mary's yes has the character of a *vow*. She is saying yes to a *permanent, spousal union* with the Holy Spirit, so that she would be of one will with God at every moment of her life.[4]

When God's will then became visible to her through the face of her Son, Mary's yes extended to wanting everything Jesus wanted and feeling everything he felt. That is why we speak of the hearts of Jesus and Mary beating in union. Jesus' joys became Mary's joys, and his Passion became her compassion.

Because she gave to God a "sincere gift of self,"[5] body and soul, Mary's entire life was taken up in that single yes. And it still is! Even now, in heaven, Mary's yes echoes and reaches down to us as and, through her continued union with the Holy Spirit, she bears the graces of her son to all who ask for them.[6]

◆ ◆ ◆

What meaning does Mary's yes have for you and me? The answer is found in that to which she said yes. She proclaimed her willingness to serve God just after the angel told her, "For with God nothing will be impossible" (Lk 1:37 RSV).

What's impossible for you right now? I'll tell you a few of the things that have, at various times, seemed impossible for me:

- feeling confident
- feeling graceful
- feeling capable
- being patient
- having self-control
- making and sustaining deep friendships
- appreciating people as themselves and not as I would like them to be
- embracing divine providence even when it hurts

None of these things comes naturally to me. I can't imagine accomplishing them all on my own strength.

I spent years grasping at straws, trying to become the kind of person I wanted to be and get the love I wanted to get by doing all the wrong things. How did I come to suspect they were the wrong things? Well, for one thing, they didn't work.

A well-known definition of insanity is "doing the same thing over and over again and expecting a different result each time." That's why popular magazines and websites, TV shows, and movies can drive you crazy. They say all you have to do is change your hairstyle, show more skin, learn a new "sex trick" (as if you were some kind of pornographic poodle), and then your ideal mate will want you.

And people fall for it. *I* fell for it. During the time when I believed I was called to marriage, I went for years thinking that if only I were prettier, more graceful, more confident, and more this or that, my future husband would fall in love with me. But no matter what I did, success was always out of reach. It was impossible. As soon as I took Mary's yes as a model, a fundamental change swept over me.

On one level, my situation remained the same: I still wanted to feel more confident, graceful, and so on, and I still believed that the qualities I desired were impossible for me to achieve through my own efforts. What changed was not so much what I was but what I was *becoming*. For the first time in my life, I felt that I was growing to be more like the woman God wanted me to be.

I used to try to change the things about myself that I didn't like, but I never really believed in my heart that I could change. It always seemed an uphill battle. Now, when I long to possess the virtues and spiritual gifts, I truly believe that all those graces, and the life changes they enable, are within my reach.

Saying yes to God's will for you means saying no to thoughts, words, and actions that separate you from him. Yet, once you do say yes, all those other things become so much smaller and unimportant by comparison.

Picture yourself as a thirsty plant. By saying yes to God and to whatever he has in store for you, you are crying out for water. Once you receive it, you will begin to bear the spiritual fruit you were meant to bear. Jesus has promised this "living water" to all who ask for it, and I have no doubt that includes you. After all, in the words of St. Paul, "all the promises of God find their Yes in him" (2 Cor 1:20 RSV).

1 0

TENDER MERCIES:
RECONNECTING WITH YOUR
VULNERABILITY

Saying yes to God is one challenge. Saying yes to a potential spouse is another. By that I mean finally letting someone under your skin—not in a pragmatic, "let's take things as they come and see how things work out" kind of way, but in a, "this is it—I'm in love, and I'm in it for the long haul" kind of way.

You may think that, if anything, you fall in love too easily. It may appear to you that unmarried people who engage in sexual intercourse do so because they're more open to a relationship than those who embrace chastity. I'm not going to deny that some single people are abstinent because they fear sexual intimacy. I call such people abstinent, not chaste, because there is no fear in chastity. However, when a single person who wants to get married instead finds himself or herself having dead-end sexual relationships, that individual is not trying to let another human being inside. That individual is trying to shut people *out*.

If you hunger for intimacy but fear rejection, it is much, much easier to let another person touch your body than to let that person touch your heart. A sex columnist for the *Village Voice* once admitted as much. "I will offer my body much sooner than my heart," Rachel Kramer Bussel wrote in her "Lusty Lady" column, "because I can walk away from casual sex, no matter how strong the connection, and not find myself crying, waiting for the phone to ring, or contemplating the other person's mindset."

Such rationalizations are all too familiar among single men and women, because they create an enticing fantasy: all you have to do is lower your expectations and you, too, can enjoy all the passion and excitement of commitment-free sexual encounters, feeling no pain from the inevitable separation.

I tried very hard to buy into that fantasy, because I believed that making myself sexually available to a man would increase the chance that he might fall in love with me. More than that, I had a sense of entitlement. I deserved a soul mate. If God wasn't keeping up his end of the bargain by sending me one, then I believed I had every right to take my pleasure where I could get it. My mentality was akin to that of a little girl who's been good for a whole day and believes that she deserves ice cream. So Mom and Dad won't take me to the ice cream shop? I'll show them! I'll get out a spoon and eat strawberry jam right out of the jar!

I admit it's possible to achieve the fantasy of casual sex with no apparent emotional consequences—just as it's possible to eat strawberry jam for three meals a day and never get cavities. In the case of the sugary foodstuff, you won't get any cavities if you eat while wearing a boxer's mouth guard. Likewise, if you make yourself available for sexual encounters outside of marriage, you won't get hurt—as long as you adopt a hard shell. But if you do that, you're opening yourself up to a painful irony.

I discovered the irony myself, late in the game: the same armor that emboldened me to be sexually available made me less attractive to the kind of man I most desired. Men with depth quickly figured out that I took sex far too lightly. Worse, I became so used to viewing myself and potential partners as objects of physical desire that I became unable to give of myself. Against my heart's own wishes, I tried to drag new relationships down to the lowest common denominator—and then wondered why the most sensitive and considerate men wouldn't stay with me.

◆ ◆ ◆

When I began to pursue chastity, recognizing how I had blunted my emotions for the sake of physical pleasure helped me gain strength to resist the temptation to revert to old behaviors.

Healing the damage takes time—but there are some fun surprises along the way. The biggest surprise for me was discovering how much there was to *like* about men. I came to notice things that I had never noticed before—intangible qualities that would never have jumped out at me when in a frame of mind where I was viewing single men only as potential dates. I began to see their thoughtfulness, their love of family, their integrity, even their vulnerability.

Later on, I would discover that my experience was not unique to women; men too, upon resolving to live chastely, have told me that their respect for women grew as a result. They began to have a more refined eye for inner beauty—the aspects of personality that, put together, add up to character. Character is the most important quality to seek in a spouse and the one that's least discussed in this day and age.

Needless to say, popular culture, obsessed as it is with materialism and superficiality, does not encourage people to build their own character, let alone to seek people who have it. Although much has been made of the sexist depictions of women in the media, men too are often presented as being little more than useful idiots. On television and in movies, if a single woman is friends with a man, the pal is more often than not a man who is identified as "gay." The message is that men who are attracted to women aren't capable of friendship or even worthy of it. In contrast, same-sex-attracted men are depicted as safe, trustworthy, nonthreatening, and giving.

Imagine if the tables were turned. Imagine watching a TV sitcom where all the same-sex-attracted men are Neanderthal blockheads, while those men not identifying as gay are kind and thoughtful, always ready to help their female friends without asking sexual favors in return. If you saw a show like that, you'd think the producers really had it out for same-sex-attracted men. Yet many women tolerate media stereotypes that elevate so-called gay characteristics because they're conditioned to expect "manly men" to lack character. Part of this conditioning comes from the media itself, but a large part of it—I'd say, most—comes from such women's own warped perspectives, brought about by the superficial nature of their dating experiences.

When I was immersed in an unchaste lifestyle, I became accustomed to seeing myself as a commodity, a varied assemblage of looks, wit, intellect, and *je ne sais quoi*. I looked for men whose commodities were worth as much as my own. Most of all, I looked for men whose commodities were readily apparent. The singles scene isn't known for its subtlety. My mindset, driven as it was by my desire to be seen as sexually attractive, forced out of the running men who were reserved or modest, who didn't flirt readily, and who weren't sufficiently attuned to the single-gal vibe that I was projecting.

Is it any surprise, then, that I tended to date narcissists and that I believed, if I let them reach me emotionally, they would hurt me? So, I built up walls of protection. I thought I was "guarding my heart." Today, I recognize those walls for what they really were—not so much walls as poorly installed weather insulation. They didn't do anything they were supposed to do. The chill winds of rejection seeped through, while the warm breezes of love were muffled.

◆ ◆ ◆

When I was thirteen, my mother and I visited London, where we took a day trip in a boat on the Thames. Every so often, the boat would have to stop at a lock. I remember the locks being like little dams. They had doors that would gradually admit water into the section of the river where we were, until the boat was level enough to glide through it to the next section. I think of being in love as like being on that Thames boat, urged along by the current, until I hit one of the locks. Then I have to wait for the water to pour in, taking me up and through to the next level. Ultimately, I keep getting farther along, and the water keeps getting deeper. But I have to get through the locks, one at a time.

Fears, like locks, can leave one feeling dead in the water. But, as the self-help slogan goes, feelings aren't facts. My mother puts it a better way: they're not the truth. The truth is always love, and love, contrary to popular belief, is not a feeling. Love is a *presence*.

Think about how we get the sun's light. From our perspective, the sun's light bends according to the hours and the seasons. Within the course of a single day, the shadow on a sundial will turn full circle. Doing a "360" is what we humans call passionate. The sun's changes may be predictable, but they're radical all the same. Yet the sun never moves. It's only because we move that its shadows appear to be so capricious.

It's the same with Jesus. He's the same yesterday, today, and forever (Heb 13:8). But how we position ourselves in relation to him can change our whole lives. Are you in a position today where, as with a plant on a windowsill at high noon, you're able to receive Jesus' direct sunlight? Or are you approaching him at an angle, letting his light hit you in some places while jealously guarding the rest of yourself in shadow?

Don't be shy. I have my shadows—lots of them. Every time I begrudge someone for making me move my bag from the subway seat next to me so he or she can sit down, that resentment is a shadow. Every time I congratulate myself on my self-control while being jealous of those who enjoy pleasures that I've forsaken, that's a shadow (two, actually—pride and envy). Every time I say or e-mail something dismissive to someone for no reason other than that she or he bugs me, that's a shadow. And every time I resent someone for being himself and not the person I want him to be, that's a shadow.

It can be hard to allow the light of Christ to dispel our shadows, partly because we're comfortable the way we are—maybe not happy but comfortable. More than that, we may not trust that Jesus could enlighten our darkness if we asked him, and the thought of his disappointing us deters us from taking the chance. But I know that when I choose to cling to my shadows, I am effectively acting on the assumption that God has the power to change some areas of my life but not others.

Could that be true? Are there really parts of my life, or anyone's life, where divine grace cannot reach? Of course not! Admittedly, God does not always give us what we want, but he *always* gives us what we need.

What's more, there are certain prayers that, to quote author Anthony DeStefano, "God always says yes to." These are prayers not for material blessings but for spiritual blessings, which God dispenses more readily and liberally than we can imagine. Here are just four of the many spiritual blessings that sacred scripture invites us to pray for:

- **Wisdom.** "For the Lord gives wisdom, from his mouth come knowledge and understanding" (Prv 2:6). "If any of you lacks wisdom, let him ask God, who gives to all men generously and without reproaching, and it will be given him" (Jas 1:5 RSV).
- **Strength.** "For this reason I kneel before the Father, from whom every family in heaven and on earth is named, that he may grant you in accord with the riches of his glory to be strengthened with power through his Spirit in the inner self" (Eph 3:14–16).
- **Hope.** "May the God of hope fill you with all joy and peace in believing, so that you may abound in hope by the power of the holy Spirit" (Rom 15:13).
- **Endurance.** "May you be strengthened with all power, according to his glorious might, for all endurance and patience with joy, giving thanks to the Father, who has qualified us to share in the inheritance of the saints in light" (Col 1:11–12 RSV).

I request those blessings in prayer every day. But most of all, I ask for the spiritual blessing that encompasses all others: recognizing and becoming part of the presence that is God's love.

◆ ◆ ◆

The word *love*, Pope Benedict XVI wrote, is "one of the most frequently used and misused of words, a word to which we attach quite different meanings."[1]

St. Thomas Aquinas observed the same thing when he wrote that, while "we are said to love a wine, or a horse, or the like," this does not carry the same meaning as when we love a person: "For it would be absurd to speak of having friendship for wine or for a horse."[2] Children recognize this absurdity early on. Say to a child, "I just love ice cream," and you can guess her response: "But would you *marry* it?"

When I speak of someone who truly loves me from the heart—whether he or she is a spouse, friend, or family member—I say that he or she "is there for me." I can't just say, "He loves me because he did x, y, and z for me," because, even though love is expressed in deeds, it cannot be measured in deeds. Someone can do things for me without loving me. But if someone truly loves me, that person is *present for me*—a presence in my life and, most of all, in my heart—and I am present for that person too.

When Isaiah prophesied Jesus' entrance into the world, he said that "the virgin shall be with child, and bear a son, and shall name him Immanuel" (Is 7:14). Immanuel is Hebrew for "God with us." It was not enough for God to merely create us. He wanted to be *with* us, to be present to us always, just as we are always present to him.

Jesus' entire life was a testament to God's loving desire to be with us—but especially his passion and death, when he literally poured out his heart to redeem us from our sins, "through him to reconcile all things for him, making peace by the blood of his cross" (Col 1:20). "This is love in its most radical form," writes Pope Benedict XVI. In contemplating the pierced heart of Jesus, "the Christian discovers the path along which his life and love must move."[3]

I encountered that "love in its most radical form" in a new way on April 13, 2006, when I made my First Communion, receiving the real presence of Jesus Christ within me for the first time. (Although Jesus' presence is not limited to the Eucharist, the Eucharist is called the real presence because, "it is presence in the fullest sense: that is to say, it is a *substantial* presence by which Christ, God and man, makes himself wholly and entirely present" [*CCC* 1374].) At the moment I received the Body of Christ, an image came to my imagination. I saw the earth as though from space; it was sheathed in a cloud of darkness. Then a patch of light broke through. It was like seeing a patch of new, healed skin emerging on a leper, and I knew with the confidence of faith that this initiation of healing would lead to still more healing. "The light shines in the darkness, and the darkness has not overcome it" (Jn 1:5).

The thought of the abiding presence of God, his Spirit ever flowing within me, is a comfort when I confront my own fears and insecurities—the Thames-like locks that prevent me from giving of myself. It helps immeasurably to know that while the locks may discourage me, the river of love exists whether I feel it or not. Most important, the locks don't go on forever. I know with all my heart that on this very river on which I sail, one day I will pass through one of them and discover that it opens up into the sea.

THE INIQUITY OF MY HEELS

I was walking home from my newspaper job late one night in 2005—so late that the Italian dessert shop on the way wasn't even open to tempt me with its fresh cannoli pastries. Traversing the dark streets in my clunky black Easy Spirit Level 2 walking shoes (Level 2 is for "advanced walkers with medium-intensity activities"), something moved me to open up my pocket Gideon's Bible to the Psalms. What I found didn't just strike me to the heart—it struck me all the way down to the soles of my shoes. Before me was Psalm 49:5 in all its King James Version glory: "Wherefore should I fear in the days of evil, when the iniquity of my heels shall compass me about?"

The time would come, a few years later, when I would have a sacred-scripture professor who barred the King James Version from his classroom because he did not deem it sufficiently accurate. Instead, he recommended the New

American Bible, Revised Edition (NABRE), which translates "the iniquity of my heels" as "the iniquity of my assailants."

I realize the NABRE does a better job of conveying the psalm's literal meaning. David feared the evil people who pursued him; perhaps he was also using poetic language to refer to the ongoing effects of his past sins, or his present temptations. Still, the Holy Spirit, working through that King James Version line about "the iniquity of my heels," led me to grasp a much-needed message, getting me thinking about certain heels of my own.

My closet, you see, did not only house comfy walking shoes. It also sheltered shoes that brought my five-foot-three frame closer to fashion-model height. Admittedly, they weren't as expensive or as frivolous as the then-fashionable *Sex and the City*–style stilettos, which had heels the diameter and length of ballpoint pens. But they still did what extra-high heels are supposed to do: alter a woman's posture, making her appear more vulnerable in every way—from the obvious way they make her teeter, bounce, and take shorter steps to the subtler ways they cause parts of her to draw in and others to stick out.

As a result, when I wore my tallest, sexiest shoes, the "iniquity of my heels" really did catch up with me. My shoes presented me as a helpless, submissive would-be sex partner. From there, they almost inevitably ended up directing my behavior. I clearly positioned myself as an object, and so I treated others as objects as well. Once you present yourself as a means to an end, you're forced to view others through that same superficial lens.

But even as the Psalmist's words reminded me of all the times I tried to squeeze into pointy-toed pumps, I knew that my true "iniquity" was not in wearing high heels. It was in what motivated me to put myself on display: an insidious fear of rejection.

◆ ◆ ◆

One day when I was five years old, my father, having been unsuccessful in his efforts to work out his differences with my mother through marriage counseling, moved out of the house. It seems strange to me now that I cannot remember seeing his bags packed. Perhaps that is because, in a way, his bags were almost always packed; his job had taken him out of town much of the time. But I do recall what it was like for my sister and me to grow up with a single mother who was haunted by her experience of a failed marriage.

My reality, from age five through my mid-twenties, was that my parents' divorce left my mother in an ongoing state of searching. At various times, she searched for God, for a man who would stay, and for her own identity. My father, having entered into a successful second marriage a year after the divorce, was comparatively stable. However, although he was never completely absent, only rarely during that time did I have the sense that he was emotionally engaged in my life.

Over time, both parents' situations would change: Mom would find faith and a lasting second marriage while Dad would make a deep and sincere effort to reach out to me. But the child is mother to the woman, and the circumstances in which we grow up determine how we react to the world. I grew up believing that marriages don't last, men come and go as they please, and the most desirable men are the least attainable.

Even as a teenager beginning to date for the first time, I wasn't stupid. I knew that my fantasy of falling in love and getting married was in conflict with the negative preconceptions I maintained against men. In fact, I even knew I had a pathological fear of rejection, a fear I harbored even before a love interest had ever rejected me. It was what I didn't know that would really hurt me.

What I didn't begin to realize until my late twenties—after enduring many breakups—was that there's a flip side to the fear of rejection. It's the fear of intimacy. Before I discovered that flip side, if you'd asked whether I feared intimacy, I would have immediately gone on the defensive. How could I be afraid of intimacy, when it was nearly always me who was dumped? If anything, I thought, my problem was not that I was distant myself but that I chose distant men. Often they were literally distant. Working in the music business, I had a knack for meeting musicians or music journalists who lived across the country or even across the ocean. That was the little recording that reverberated in my head all the years I played the dating game: intimacy isn't my problem; it's *theirs*.

Finally, when I was twenty-nine and going through yet another painful breakup with yet another long-distance boyfriend, something changed within me as a new intuition arose. Although it would be some time yet before the light of grace would lead me to change my lifestyle, I slowly began to realize I was sabotaging my own dreams.

◆ ◆ ◆

Every so often, if you listen to your conscience, it will tell you something that you've really known all along but were unwilling to admit to yourself.

I listened to my conscience that day when I was hurting, and it told me why nearly all my relationships had been so brief—why I'd allowed myself to use men and be used in return. It said that I had a fear of intimacy. The fear, I realized, stemmed from the knowledge that if I let a man get under my skin, I would become vulnerable to the crushing blow of rejection.

In that light, thinking back on dating experiences that had seemed so spontaneous and passionate, the experiences suddenly became visible for what they were: cold, clinical couplings. They weren't really about excitement. They were about control.

I began to see how, despite my longing for closeness, when the opportunity for intimacy actually arose I couldn't take the risk. Being convinced in my heart that a breakup was always inevitable, it had seemed that the best way to protect myself was to speed up the entire relationship.

Since I knew that a man wouldn't take me seriously if I rushed into physical intimacy, I would do just that. That way, when I left his apartment, I would know there was no need to leave any things of mine behind. There would be no uncertainty. The pain of separation would come, but it wouldn't hit me so deeply, because I'd see it coming.

As time passed, and especially after my conversion to Catholicism at the age of thirty-seven spurred me to pursue chastity, that insight would prove to be the leading edge of my healing. No longer could I put the blame on others for my loneliness. Instead, in the words of cartoonist Walt Kelly, "We have met the enemy and he is us."

◆ ◆ ◆

In the wake of my conversion, the light of faith, and the moral demands it placed upon me, helped me resist using the temptation to use physical intimacy to end relationships before they could really begin. But if I were truly going to counter my fear of rejection, I could not merely put an end to unhealthy behaviors; I had to pursue *healthy* behaviors.

Part of that effort required getting help from a Catholic therapist, which I especially needed since my problems had roots in childhood experiences of abuse and loss.[1] But it wasn't enough to learn how to act from a healthy *intellectual* place; I also had to learn how to act from a healthy *spiritual* place. That meant going to confession regularly, getting into the habit of daily Mass, and finding a spiritual director.[2]

Of those three spiritual practices, the one that was hardest to get the hang of was regular confession. Daily Mass was a difficult discipline to develop, but its mental

and spiritual benefits were obvious. Even the most secular doctor will tell you that a good treatment for anxi-
ety is "meditation." Well, a weekday Mass provides a half
hour of quiet meditation, plus union with the body, blood,
soul, and divinity of Jesus Christ. Other things might bring
greater sensations of pleasure—since grace is not something
a person feels with the senses—but nothing could bring
deeper inner joy. And I could also appreciate the benefit of
a spiritual director—a priest who knew my strengths and
weaknesses, and could help me recognize and cooperate
with the Holy Spirit's action in my heart.

But what about going to confession regularly, as in
once a month or more? Intellectually, I had a sense that it
was something worth doing; I wanted to stay right with
God. But I couldn't get a feel for confession as I did for
other practices of the Catholic faith. I saw it simply as an
obligation, something I did because it was good for me,
such as eating my vegetables and taking long walks in my
Level two shoes—not because it felt good.

All that changed in February 2007 when an extraordinary event served to lift the veil from the Sacrament of
Reconciliation, revealing the action of Christ empower-
ing the words spoken by the priest. I was then on staff at
the New York *Daily News*, where Sunday was an ordinary
workday. On this particular Sunday, as I went to Mass at
the church across the street from the *News*, I was thinking
about how I would be giving a talk on chastity that evening
at St. Joseph's in Greenwich Village. Although I did not
have grave sin on my conscience, the thought of preaching
morality in a neighborhood where I had, not so long ago,
been immersed in a worldly lifestyle made me conscious
of the need to be in a state of grace. So, after Mass, I asked
the priest to hear my confession.

When I finished confessing, the priest assigned me
my penance: ten minutes of prayer before the Blessed Sacrament. And he added, almost to himself, "It isn't really a

penance." I had to agree; visiting our Lord in the Eucharist is an undiluted joy. But it was time for me to be in the newsroom, so I dashed across Thirty-Third Street, resolving to fulfill the penance that evening before my talk at St. Joseph's.

And so it was that I arrived at the Greenwich Village church at about 7:00 p.m., half an hour before I was to speak, settled into a pew upfront, and checked the time on my cell phone so as to start the clock on my ten-minute penance. Not being used to silent prayer, and not yet having gotten into the habit of praying the Rosary, I wasn't sure what to do. So I fished out of my purse a small book of Catholic prayers and prayed ten minutes' worth of the Act of Faith, Act of Hope, Act of Love, Prayer to St. Michael, Guardian Angel Prayer, Our Father, Hail Mary, and Miraculous Medal prayer, Memorare—you name it, I prayed it.

Amazingly, after all those prayers, my cell phone showed that there was still a couple of minutes left, so I added petitions for myself and my loved ones. Saying them while kneeling before the tabernacle seemed to give them more meaning.

None of this would be remarkable were it not for what happened the following morning in the newsroom. My work phone rang; it was my father. Dad is the calmest person I have ever met in my life. So, when he has a certain edge to his voice, an edge that makes it sound as though he is making an *effort* to be calm, I know something is wrong. His voice had that edge as he greeted me. I braced myself for bad news.

My father told me that a relative, someone very dear to me, was in the hospital. She had taken ill the night before— so ill that she stopped breathing and had to be revived with CPR. Thankfully she was now getting the care she needed and was expected to make a full recovery (which she did). But it was a very close call and would likely have been fatal if she had not gotten medical assistance in time.

As Dad spoke, it hit me that this woman whom I so loved had been stricken shortly before I did my penance. Right at the time that she nearly died, I was praying before the Blessed Sacrament. At that moment, it seemed to me as though a veil were briefly lifted so that the mysteries of divine providence became clear: if I had not received my not-really-a-penance penance, I would not have been by the tabernacle, praying for my loved ones, including this very relative at the very moment when she needed prayer.

This new insight into God's loving plan changed the way I looked at confession. Before, I had seen it only in a "me and Jesus" kind of way. It was purely about restoring the vertical relationship between myself and God. But seeing how the Lord used my confession as an occasion to bring me into prayer for a loved one who, at that exact moment, was desperately in need of it, I realized for the first time that reconciliation with God was *not just about me*. It was about receiving the opportunity from the Father to cooperate in his Son's "ministry of reconciliation" (2 Cor 5:18)—putting something *good* into the world, to help make up for the bad things I had put in.

That is how I came to understand for myself the words of the *Catechism*, which stresses, "Forgiveness of sins brings reconciliation with God, but also with the Church" (CCC 1462). The *Catechism* also quotes St. Joan of Arc, who testified to her judges, "About Jesus Christ and the Church, I simply know they're just one thing, and we shouldn't complicate the matter" (CCC 795). It is through the Church, his Mystical Body, that Jesus extends his reign over all creation (CCC 792). For that reason, in the words of St. John Paul II, "this reconciliation with God [through confession] leads, as it were, to other reconciliations, which repair the other breaches caused by sin. The forgiven penitent is reconciled with himself in his inmost being, where he regains his innermost truth. He is reconciled with his brethren whom he has in some way offended and wounded. He is reconciled with the Church. He is reconciled with all creation" (CCC 1469).

Even though my relative was not a member of the Church, she was yet part of God's creation, living—whether she realized it or not—under the headship of Christ, who loved her as a potential member of his Mystical Body.[3] For that reason, when I was reconciled to the Mystical Body of Christ through my confession, my prayers for her took on renewed power thanks to the sacrament having removed obstacles between me and God's grace.

Realizing all this gave me great joy. I phoned a seminarian friend and, after asking his prayers for my loved one's recovery, told him the story of the penance I had been given that led to my prayer at the time that illness struck.

"Right priest, right time," he said.

After a moment's pause, he exclaimed, "God is so good! If he were running for office, I'd vote for Him!"

◆ ◆ ◆

The longer you're out of a relationship, the easier it becomes to forget that your ability to enter a relationship is dependent on your ability to get over your fear. It sounds like a paradox, and to some extent it is; being attracted to someone includes in its nature the desire not to be separated from that person. Yet, it's possible to cultivate a fear of rejection to the point where the fear itself becomes larger than life, as though it were a third party in the relationship. ("Hi, this is my boyfriend Mark, and that big shadow next to us is my Looming Sensation of Impending Rejection. I call it Loomis for short.") And the more you hold onto that fear, the lonelier you become.

During the period when I was adjusting to life as a single Catholic, there were times when, however much I tried to act as if I had overcome my fear of rejection, the fear persisted. The wiser I pretended to be, the more the iniquity of my heels encompassed me.

When it comes down to it, once you become dissatisfied with your own behavior, only two things will give you the wisdom and motivation to make necessary changes: time and prayer.

After mentioning "heels" in Psalm 49, the psalmist proclaims with confidence, "God will ransom my soul from the power of Sheol, for he will receive me" (Ps 49:15 RSV). I take that and other promises to mean he begins his redemptive work on me while I'm on this side of the grave, molding me into his likeness and transforming my weakness into strength.

God also says to pray always and not to lose heart (Lk 18:1). Perhaps that's his way of keeping me on my toes.

HOW BEGINNINGS SHAPE
ENDINGS

Do you ever have one of those moments when you say something that makes perfect sense to you, but the person you're addressing has absolutely no idea what you mean? It happened to me in late 2003, on one of my first dates after I began to get serious about chastity. I was saying goodbye to my date—also a believer—after we had what I thought was a pleasant lunch. It was our second time out together, and I hoped we would meet again. However, I became confused when he gave me what I thought were conflicting signals. He seemed to want to keep all his options open—not planning to see me again but not ruling it out either.

I commented that, at that point in my life, I believed I should start every relationship as though it were going to resolve into marriage—and I totally lost him. I think it must have sounded as if I *intended* every relationship to end in marriage, as though I showed up for every date with absolute certainty that "this man is The One." Of course that would be unwise and, from my date's perspective perhaps even downright creepy.

I tried to explain to my date that I meant I was seeking to avoid doing anything at the beginning of a relationship that I would later regret. Even if some tactic were to help me win a husband, if it involved dishonesty, disrespect, playing games, or a lack of sexual restraint, it would not be something I would look back upon fondly after years of marriage.

In the New York City area where I was living at the time, as with many urban areas with a large pool of single adults, the model for relationships for many people was that they became physically intimate to see if they wanted to be committed. It's the, "let's have fun and see if it turns into something" philosophy. Underlying it is the old Freudian conceit that people have sexual "needs," and that these needs can exist either on their own or as the prelude to a relationship, but that it is unnatural to prioritize other types of intimacy ahead of them.

Although I myself do have these "needs"—or, more accurately, desires—in the deepest part of me, I never really wanted to place them before emotional intimacy. I don't think it's natural for people to operate that way unless they have serious problems with intimacy, as I did—and even then, I don't think it makes them truly happy.

Once I determined to no longer be a hopeless fish in New York City's sea of singles but instead a little Christian Ichthus swimming against the current, self-restraint became a priority, as did honesty, respect, and not playing games. Those last three in particular seem obvious, but they go against the nature of dating in a sophisticated urban social world that encourages men and women to hide their true feelings from one another.

Given hindsight, when my date was confused with my remark about starting each relationship as though it would resolve into marriage, I could have expressed what I meant to say by drawing a circle. If someone asks you to draw a circle and you consent, you don't get cagey and pretend at first that you're going to draw a square. It messes the whole thing up. If you're a man or woman of your word, you have to start the circle with the same steady curve with which it ends, because once you've started it, there's no way to go back and correct the beginning.

Likewise, it's practically impossible to draw a perfect circle without a compass, and it's impossible to start a relationship leading to marriage without a moral compass. In fact, without a compass, it's even harder to draw a perfect heart.

◆ ◆ ◆

There was a time that when a man and woman entered into a new relationship, the decisions they faced were over whether to make it exclusive and, after that, whether to get engaged. Today, given the same situation, the first decision for many—in fact, most, not counting those who actively practice a religious faith—is whether the time is right to engage in sexual intercourse. Romance, by contrast, is seen as something that must happen by itself, without a conscious decision. Any attempt to introduce an element of choice into it is seen as decidedly unromantic.

Now, the most obvious problem with relying on impulse is that it doesn't work. In fact, as soon as we buy into the idea that we "fall" in love, we're at a deficit. Falling implies something you do accidentally, without even trying, while true love requires an act of will.

This point about the nature of love happens to be a truth of philosophy, not only faith, making it one of the issues on which we as Catholics can find ground with pagan thinkers. Even twentieth-century psychologist Erich Fromm, who believed that salvation was to be found not in Jesus Christ but in Karl Marx, saw that it would be more accurate to call the experience of "falling in love" *standing in love*.[1]

Despite the general atmosphere that encourages us to give in to passing feelings rather than put in the hard work to build a lifetime commitment, on some level our culture is aware that love involves a decision. We speak of "opening up" our hearts to new loves, or we say a friend has "closed her heart" to a former boyfriend. We have a sense, however vague, that love involves the opening of a door.

There is indeed a door in the heart. Behind it is love that flows like a river. Its source is God—because God is love.

◆ ◆ ◆

I am speaking now to you if you feel called to marriage rather than celibacy, and sharing with you what I wish someone had shared with me. If you really love, you choose to open the door of your heart, making a conscious decision to admit the love you long to feel inside your heart for one special person. The decision has to be conscious, because no matter how irresistible the attraction, you must choose whether or not to take on the responsibility of giving yourself fully to another. You know that the love behind the door entails responsibility, because you know that it is for life.

Now, here's the exciting part. This great love to which you have access is meant to be shared in a sexual way with only one person—and that's for a reason. God created marriage as a means to make human beings more like him. The greatest way we can be like God is to love one another the way he loves us. And how are we to imagine God's love for us? St. John Chrysostom, drawing from sacred scripture, offers the beautiful insight that each of us should think of God's gifts, which have been bestowed on everyone alike, as if they were bestowed on himself alone: "For as if speaking of himself alone, Paul writes to the Galatians (2:20): 'Christ . . . loved me and delivered Himself for me.'"[2]

In other words, God wants you to be able to love one human being the way he loves you, as though you were the only person in the world. From there, he means to shape you further. In the deepest spiritual way, you are meant to spread the love that you share with your spouse to every human being with whom you come into contact—and ultimately, through prayer, charity, and Catholic social action, with the whole world.

This is why Christians believe that marriage is more than just a check box on the census form. It's a spiritual *vocation*. Those of us who long for it are called to it. It is a participation in Jesus' own spiritual vocation as Bridegroom of the Church. Priests and others who are living vocations of celibacy for the kingdom are sharing in their same vocation, only they are participating in Jesus' spiritual fruitfulness, while the married participate both in his spiritual fruitfulness and in his physical fruitfulness as Creator.[3]

Knowing this sheds new light on the way St. John describes our relationship with God: "We love because he first loved us" (1 Jn 4:19). We are able to choose marriage because God chose us for marriage—and this is true on two levels. Through calling us to union with his Church, he espouses us to himself as his beloved bride (CCC 796); through calling us to union with an earthly spouse, he shows us how to make of our own lives a sign of his fruitful love.

We publicly acknowledge our yes to marital love in our "I do's." The promises to be true in good times and in bad, in sickness and in health, and to love and honor one another all the days of our life are the words tradition uses to remind us of the responsibilities contained within our assent. Yet, we know that the marriage vows are not really the beginning of our yes.

C. S. Lewis wrote that those who get to heaven will realize, once they arrive, that they have in a sense always been there—that their experience of it began on earth.[4]

Likewise, when you enter marriage, you will know that your yes to love began well before your "I do."

In the same way that arriving in heaven will cause those who are there to understand how heaven's seeds were planted long ago in their earthly lives, so too can the experience of marriage, with its joys and continual self-sacrifice, bring a deeper understanding of the nature of godly love. Through the grace of the sacrament, "being rooted and grounded in love, [you] may have power to comprehend with all the saints what is the breadth and length and height and depth, and to know the love of Christ which surpasses knowledge, that you may be filled with all the fulness of God" (Eph 3:17–19 RSV).

◆ ◆ ◆

The rich spousal metaphors that appear in the Old and New Testaments, show us that marital love, bringing husband and wife into a union of complete self-gift, is a symbol of God's love. But more than that, it *is* God's love. In the Sacrament of Matrimony, "the spouses receive the Holy Spirit as the communion of love of Christ and the Church. The Holy Spirit is the seal of their covenant, the ever available source of their love and the strength to renew their fidelity" (CCC 1624).

Yet, while marital love is meant to model God's love in a special way, it is by no means the only goal to which those called to marriage are to aspire. This most deeply felt longing with which we are created, the desire to be complemented by another, has a purpose in and of itself. That purpose has deep meaning, enough to transform each one of us and, if we would follow it as far as it would lead us, everyone we touch.

If you are indeed called to marriage, then, as strange as it may seem, the purpose that sets your heart afire and makes you long for spousal union will not—in fact, cannot—be satisfied by setting marriage as your main goal.

The *single-minded* pursuit of marriage can actually draw you farther away from completion and happiness. That may sound like a troublesome paradox, but behind it is a liberating truth.

In Lewis Carroll's *Through the Looking-Glass*, the chess-themed sequel to *Alice's Adventures in Wonderland*, Alice at one point sees the Red Queen and tries to walk over to her—only to discover that, since the laws of physics are upended in Wonderland, she is actually headed *away* from the monarch. So she decides to take a different tack, walking in the opposite direction from the queen instead of toward her. Sure enough, within a minute, she finds herself face-to-face with the regal chess piece.

Like Alice, you who are seeking a spouse have a goal in mind. To fulfill it, you have a walk—a direction for your life. Yet the more you walk in the direction of finding a lifetime love, the farther you may find yourself from your goal. That's because walking toward a mere object is not really a walk—it's a hunt.

A hunt, as we all know, generally winds up with something getting killed. If your object is love, the nature of the hunt means that once you find it, it's going to die. Only it won't die from a bullet; it'll die of starvation. No matter how much you may tell yourself that you want to give all your love to a spouse, the hunter's mentality that you've bought into is centered around taking, not giving.

Does that all sound strange coming from someone who believes in the goodness of Holy Matrimony? It shouldn't.

Recall my friend Paraic Maher's definition of chastity: "The virtue that enables us to love fully and completely in every relationship, in the manner that is appropriate to the relationship." Loving fully in a marital relationship includes the marital act—sexual union—so of course it is essential that the person you marry is someone who attracts you on every level: mind, body, and spirit. But when we hunt for the "perfect" mate, we set our sights on what another person can *do* for us, instead of what we are to *be* for others. The healthier approach, both psychologically and spiritually, is to focus primarily on learning to "love fully and completely in every relationship, in the manner appropriate to the relationship"—and only *secondarily* on keeping your eyes open for the one you are destined to love as a spouse.

To be able to love, you have to give, and to be a true giver, you have to give to all—to both those who are close to you and those who aren't. "For if you love those who love you, what reward have you?" (Mt 5:46 RSV). There is a real reward in this life from giving without discriminating. It shapes you into the person God wants you to be. As Charlie Kaufman wrote in his screenplay for *Adaptation*, "You are what you love, not what loves you."

This love is the moral compass that will enable you to both begin a relationship and bring it around to a perfect circle. The Greek word for it is *agape* (pronounced a-GAH-pay). It's the word St. John used when he wrote, "God is love" (1 Jn 4:8). In the words of modern writer Peter Kreeft, "It means loving people not just in terms of justice or what they deserve, but simply loving them absolutely."[5] Forget falling in love or even standing in love; as Kreeft puts it, we *rise* in *agape*.

If you take that longing you feel in your heart and direct it toward sharing *agape* love with those around you, then you will never again have to worry about the million things that could go wrong in a budding relationship. None of those things will matter, because you will have a divine spark in your heart that will outshine all the externals. The spouse whom divine providence has in store for you will be drawn to that spark—and will carry that same spark within, for you will both draw light from the same Source.

13

ANSWERING THE CALL

A certain seminarian—I'll call him J.—told me about the one time during seminary when he began to have doubts about his vocation. It happened when he was listening to a visiting speaker who had given the seminarians a talk intended to strengthen them in their resolve. Unfortunately, it had the opposite effect for this young man.

The speaker, a married layman, informed the seminarians, who were then in their initial year of studies, that before discerning the diocesan priesthood they should first discern whether they had a call to marriage or to consecrated celibacy. Only if they were certain they were *first* called to celibacy, he said, could they have a true vocation to the diocesan priesthood. He based his claim on a line in the *Catechism*: "All the ordained ministers of the Latin Church, with the exception of permanent deacons, are normally chosen from among men of faith who live a celibate life and who intend to remain *celibate* 'for the sake of the kingdom of heaven'" (CCC 1579).[1]

Those words brought J. to a vocational crisis. Until that moment, he had thought Christ was calling him to be "a priest forever" (Heb 7:17). He had only just entered seminary and was doing everything he could to follow God's will for him, including living the discipline of celibacy. The idea of remaining celibate for the rest of his life did not sound easy, but it seemed possible with the help of grace. Was he now to drop out of seminary because he had not felt called to celibacy *first*, before he had even discerned his call to the priesthood?

A talk with his spiritual director restored J.'s peace. The priest explained to him that, however well-intentioned the visiting speaker was, he was mistaken about the role of grace in the call to a vocation that requires celibacy.

The message the spiritual director shared is what I would like to share now with you, in my own words. When it comes to vocation, no one, and I mean *no one*, is called to celibacy as their one and only calling. The literal meaning of celibacy is "unmarried," and vocation, like chastity itself, is always something positive; it cannot be defined simply by what it is not. So celibacy in the vocational sense is always part of something more, such as priesthood, consecrated life, or a life given to apostolic work.

Yes, there are men who, while not belonging to religious orders, make private vows or promises of consecrated celibacy, and there are women who do so as well (I am one), including consecrated virgins. But I think if you talked to any one of them and asked, "When did you realize your vocation was to be celibate," he would very quickly tell you that his *vocation* is not celibacy. Rather, he has a celibate *vocation*. There is a difference. The difference is that a vocation is a positive call to give your entire self—mind, body, and spirit—in the way that will most glorify God, according to the disposition and gifts that you have been given.

In the Catholic Church, it has always been recognized that most people are given disposition and gifts by which they may best glorify God through giving themselves to him through marriage and parenthood. By marrying, having children, and raising their children in the faith, they build up the Body of Christ both physically and spiritually.[2]

Others, a smaller group, are called to glorify God in a way that is not mediated by a spouse—which is to say, in a vocation that requires celibacy. That life may be one of contemplative prayer, an active apostolate, or—for men called to act in the person of Christ at the altar—the priesthood. The important thing is that, with every celibate vocation, the primary question for the discerner is not, "Is God calling me not to have sex?" Rather, the primary question is, "Is God calling me to glorify him in this particular vocation of personal consecration, religious life, or priesthood?"

That is the primary question, because celibacy is not the primary call of any vocation. It belongs rather to the *fulfillment* of the primary call, which is always first and foremost a call to holiness.[3]

When we say yes to God's call, we are cooperating with his will to bring to fruition the graces we received in our Baptism. Every yes brings more grace. J.'s spiritual director brought him back to a sense of peace by assuring him that if God was truly calling him to the priesthood, then God would not fail to reward his yes with all the grace he needed to fulfill his vocation, including the grace to live the discipline of celibacy.

I speak from experience. Two and a half years ago, after believing for my whole life that I was called to marriage, I came to realize that God was asking me to say yes to a celibate vocation.

My vocation did not come to me by way of resignation. I did not say to myself, "No man wants me, so I might as well make a vow and have done with it." The recognition came instead as a sense of recognition that, without my even realizing it, God had been calling me all along to do the kind of work for the kingdom—as a writer and speaker on spiritual healing, as a student of theology, and as (I hope) a professor—that required a complete gift of self.

I realized I had to make a choice. Did I want marriage so badly that I was willing to make whatever sacrifices were necessary for the good of married life? Did I want marriage if it meant sacrificing my dreams of teaching and of reaching victims of trauma and abuse with the healing love of Christ?

The answer for me was that I would rather sacrifice my hopes and dreams of married love than sacrifice the work I was doing for the Kingdom, work to which I felt I was called. So I made my choice. It was not easy, but I am not sorry. Each day brings more reasons to be thankful for the providence of God that has led me to a sense of growing intimacy with him, an intimacy that remains even in times of loneliness and suffering.

The words of St. Josemaría Escrivá to women living celibacy for the kingdom—he calls it "apostolic celibacy"—speak to my experience and to the experience of the many celibate Catholics I am blessed to know: "People who follow a vocation to apostolic celibacy are not old maids who do not understand or value love; on the contrary, their lives can only be explained in terms of this divine Love (I like to write it with a capital letter), which is the very essence of every Christian vocation."[4]

14

THE GIFT OF THE PRESENT
MOMENT

There is perhaps no experience more like being buried alive than undergoing a closed MRI. I was reminded of this when I had one such full-body scan in anticipation of a surgical procedure. I could not move. My throat seemed to close up, as it can at times when I am lying on my back and have trouble swallowing. I had to keep my eyes shut, as the nearness of the MRI's surface made it seem as though the machine was swallowing me up like Jonah's whale.

When I made the appointment for the test, the receptionist had advised me to bring a favorite recording. Now, as I lay in the belly of the machine wearing clunky, industrial-style headphones, the technician began to pipe in the music I had brought: Handel's *Messiah*. It came through the headphone speakers sounding faint and tinny, like an angelic broadcast from a far-off planet—until it was eclipsed by the scanner's buzzsaw-like din.

I thought that I knew just from my everyday life experiences what it was like to be alone, until I discovered inside
that fiberglass sarcophagus what it was really like. The only
thing I could do to remember I was not truly isolated was
to send prayers up to Jesus through Mary, using a ring-style
finger rosary, which the technician had kindly let me take
into the machine. I know it helped, because the thought of
Jesus' love flowing back to me through Mary made tears
run down the sides of my cheeks. Then I had to stop myself
from crying, for fear that my breathing passages really
would close up.

I remember, back when I longed for faith, reading science-fiction novels by Philip K. Dick in which the author,
who suffered from schizophrenia complicated by drugs,
envisioned worlds where people were so isolated that their
prayers could not reach God.

As an agnostic, the idea that one could long for a God
who really did exist, and yet be unable to reach him, struck
me as peculiarly terrifying—more frightening even than
the idea that there was no God. And, in a strange way, I
think that Dick's dark vision, even though it was based on
the Gnostic heresy, helped fuel my longing for a God who
could be reached—the longing that would eventually open
the door to let him reach me.

◆ ◆ ◆

A Dominican friar has told me that the root of "monk," the
Greek *monos*, means not just "alone" or "single," as it is
usually translated, but also "alone with."

For me, living as a chaste, unmarried woman in the
world, that insight points to what is at once the greatest
blessing and the greatest challenge of earthly life. There is
really no such thing as being alone, because we are always
in the presence of God. But, since we are spirit and flesh, it
is this very spiritual presence of the God we cannot see that

makes us long for the physical presence of another person. And yet, even when we have the love of another person, our love—if it is as it should be—ultimately makes us long still more for the physical presence of the infinitely loving Christ. Even when we seek the love of another person, in some sense, at the bottom of our desire to find fulfillment, we are really seeking God with skin on.

I believe it is important to remember that fact, because I have met unmarried young Catholic adults who long so much to have a husband or wife that they feel that what they do on a daily basis—their job or studies—is not really meaningful. They feel that whatever they do, they are only treading water until the person arrives who will give their life purpose and enable them to enter into their true, married vocation.

That is wrong. If your job or your studies, or whatever you choose to do with your time and talents, does not have meaning right at this moment, it will not suddenly have meaning when Mr. or Miss Right comes along. Your ultimate vocation may very well be marriage. But right now, at this moment, your vocation is to be a single person living within the "now and not yet" that lies between grace and glory.

If there is one thing I could have done differently during my first few years as a Catholic, when I was hoping for marriage, that is it. I spent a lot of time pursuing, or trying to be pursued by, prospective husbands, when I should have been pursuing the one thing sacred scripture tells me is the will of God for my life: my sanctification (see 1 Thes 4:3).

It is not that I avoided worship; I went to Mass, confessed regularly, and sought spiritual direction. But I thought that whatever I was doing at the moment in my work, studies, or apostolate was far less important than whatever I would do once I had my "true married vocation." As a result, I did not put my full heart into the work of the present day, and so did not accept the gift of the present moment.

In my journey toward a deeper faith, I have learned that, although I hope for joy in heaven, I cannot treat the here and now as though it were unimportant. If that were my life, I would go crazy. We already have a "waiting room" in Catholic theology, and it is called purgatory. Life cannot be an interminable holding pattern.

Looking back, I can pick out the day when I began to realize that, whatever my vocation might be (and I was still hoping for marriage), God's plan for me was not some vague mystery of the future. It was, rather, unfolding in the present moment; if I wanted to cooperate with it, I had to pay attention. That day was April 21, 2009, when I visited the Polish town of Oświęcim—better known under its German name, Auschwitz.

◆ ◆ ◆

Writing about chastity can put one in the oddest situations. In all my years as a rock journalist, I never thought I would be touring Poland—let alone with a vowed celibate man constantly at my side. Yet, there I was, on a minibus traveling from Krakow to Auschwitz, next to my "road manager," as I affectionately called him—Brother Benedykt, a Polish Dominican friar in his mid-twenties, just weeks away from ordination to the priesthood. His order's publishing house had just published The Thrill of the Chaste (its Polish title, I was told, meant literally "The Shiver of Chastity"), and it had fallen to him to make sure I was where I needed to be during my five-day speaking tour of the country.

It was a beautiful sunny day—almost too beautiful, I thought, for a visit to perhaps the most somber place on earth. Since I had free time before my talk that evening in Krakow, Brother Benedykt had agreed to travel with me on the forty-five-minute ride to the Auschwitz Memorial and

Museum, the site of the concentration camp where more than one million Jews were put to death, as well as many thousands of Polish Catholics and others targeted by the Nazis during World War II.

Having been raised Jewish, I had always thought of Auschwitz as holy ground. On this day, however, my thoughts were centered on two of the Catholics martyred there: my fellow Jewish convert St. Teresa Benedicta of the Cross (born Edith Stein) and St. Maximilian Kolbe.

Since it was St. Maximilian's intercession that led me into the Church, I especially wanted to see the place where the humble Franciscan priest offered up his life so that a condemned fellow prisoner might live to be reunited with his wife and children. The minibus ride passed quickly as I imagined what it would be like to stand where he had stood and thank him for being an instrument of God on my behalf. It seemed to me almost as though the saint himself were bringing me to visit his place of martyrdom, for, had he not aided my conversion with his prayers, I would not even be speaking on chastity in Poland.

There was just one thing missing, I reflected. I like to be near relics of my patron saints, for relics are a privileged means that God uses to bring us closer to the saints' prayerful presence. But there were no relics of St. Maximilian at Auschwitz. The Nazis cremated his remains. After his death, all that anyone could find of his body were some hairs of his beard that a forward-thinking barber had secretly preserved during his lifetime. I did not know where they were kept but knew I would not find them at the camp's site.[1]

As the minibus approached Auschwitz, Brother Benedykt and I could see large crowds of people, including numerous groups of schoolchildren. The minibus dropped us off a short walk from the former camp, and we followed the crowd to the entrance. But as we got close enough to the wrought-iron gates to read the grimly deceptive motto forged into them—"*Arbeit macht frei*" ("Work makes you free")—we were stopped by a guard who asked us for our tickets.

We were confused; since when did the museum require tickets? The guard, who spoke English, explained that tickets were required for security purposes one day a year, Holocaust Remembrance Day—which, as fate would have it, was the very day of our visit.

No amount of pleading could make the guard let us in; we simply didn't have the needed security clearance. Finally, Brother Benedykt and I turned around and walked toward the nearby town of Oświęcim, hoping to find something to see that would make the trip worthwhile.

I remember that, as we began heading away from the camp, Brother Benedykt said, "I am very sad. I wanted to show you the camp." He felt personally responsible for the disappointment.

Is it possible to surprise one's self? The words that came out of my mouth weren't what I would have imagined I would say in such a situation. I began predictably enough: "Don't feel bad . . ." But then I thought for a moment and found myself choking up. "I mean . . . this situation is so unusual, that I can't feel bad about it," I said, "because it's so obviously the will of God."

And it really was, I realized. The knowledge was strangely consoling. Tears started trickling down my face, but I couldn't tell how much they were due to sadness and how much they were due to joy.

Brother Benedykt began to apologize again. I interrupted him. "It's really not bad. It's actually kind of beautiful. I mean, how often in life can I really be sure that where I am right now, at this moment, is where God most wants me to be? Well, right now, despite my best efforts, I cannot be where *I* want to be—so I must be where he wants me to be. And that is something beautiful.

"Looking back," I went on, "I can remember moments like this, when I tried as hard as I could to get something I wanted, and my best efforts weren't good enough. And when I think about those moments now, I realize that my life didn't stay unhappy. Things got better. Back when, even after asking St. Maximilian's intercession, I still lost my job at the *New York Post*, I thought that losing my job was the worst thing that could happen to me. But today I can actually be thankful for what happened, because if I hadn't been fired, I wouldn't have written *The Thrill of the Chaste*, and I wouldn't be here today.

"So," I concluded, "maybe this too is a case where God is saying 'no' to one of my desires only so that I'll be where he wants me to be when he says 'yes' to something I want even more."

My words didn't seem to assuage Brother Benedykt's feelings of responsibility. But we kept walking, and, not long after I dried my tears, we reached a Carmelite convent. Seeing it, my thoughts turned to St. Teresa Benedicta, who was a Carmelite, and I was thankful to be so close to where she made her final sacrifice. A Carmelite nun stood in the parking lot of the convent, speaking to a lady in her seventies who had a little white lap dog on a leash. Brother Benedykt approached the nun and said something to her in Polish. The nun said something to the lady, and before I knew it, Brother Benedykt was beckoning to me.

"There is a church in town that is dedicated to Maximilian Kolbe and Edith Stein," he said. "This lady says she knows the priest and is willing to take us there."

And so it was that Brother Benedykt and I found ourselves in the back seat of the lady's car, which was like being in a limousine (she was apparently well-to-do, having her own driver). Arriving at the church, we were greeted by the pastor, who showed us fine artworks representing Kolbe and Stein's life stories. It was like being in a museum.

Finally, the priest showed us into the sacristy. Nothing could have prepared me for what I found there.

If you have been inside a sacristy, you may know that it is the part of the church where relics are usually stored—and the church is most likely to have relics of its own patron. Before me, in elegant reliquaries, were items that had belonged to St. Maximilian. There was a rosary that he had given to a fellow prisoner at Auschwitz who, as with the Polish soldier whose life Kolbe saved, survived the death camp. There was a tiny booklet containing the prayers of the Office for the Dead, handmade from scraps of paper inscribed in ink. Kolbe had asked an artistically gifted prisoner to craft the booklet so he could pray in secret for the repose of the souls of his fellow prisoners. And there was a miniature metal chalice, small enough to be concealed in the palm of one's hand, that Kolbe had used to celebrate a clandestine Mass that his fellow inmates risked their lives to attend.

Looking at the contents of these reliquaries and thinking of how they were part of St. Maximilian's life, I had the feeling of being in the saint's presence. But there was yet a fourth reliquary, one that made my joy complete. It displayed a white piece of paper, upon which were attached several black hairs, remnants of Kolbe's beard.

As I venerated the relics, praying for St. Maximilian to continue interceding for me, my thoughts returned to the moment earlier that day, when Brother Benedykt and I had been turned away from the Auschwitz gates. I cried again, this time only out of joy. "Thank you, Lord, for the times when you said 'no.' Thank you for not giving me what I thought I wanted. This is what I truly want, Lord—this moment that you are giving me right now."

◆ ◆ ◆

Toward the end of his life, St. Thomas Aquinas had a mysterious experience while celebrating Mass, after which he could no longer write. When his secretary urged him to resume composing his *Summa Theologiae*, the saint is said to have responded, "All that I have hitherto written seems to me nothing but straw."

It is tantalizing to imagine what sort of insight could possibly have made the Angelic Doctor believe that all his work was worthless. I wonder sometimes whether he was granted a vision of a truth that was both extremely simple and extraordinarily profound. Especially, I wonder if he saw, in a flash, how God saves us from *not being*. For we exist only insofar as we exist in him.

When I was a child growing up Jewish, if a holiday fell on the Sabbath, my mother would say a certain ancient Hebrew prayer while lighting Shabbat candles. Following tradition, she would say this same prayer at a meal when serving a fruit that had just come into season. The prayer is called the *Shehecheyanu*, and in English it says, "Blessed are You, Lord our God, King of the Universe, who has granted us life, sustained us and enabled us to reach this present time."

Hearing my mother pray the *Shehecheyanu*, and learning to pray it with her, helped me to think about the gift of changing times and seasons. I think about it even more as a Catholic. Leave it to T. S. Eliot's fictional J. Alfred Prufrock to measure out his life with coffee spoons. I measure out my life with palm fronds, blessed candles, and Easter lilies.

15

LIVING MODESTLY

One afternoon, shortly after the first edition of *The Thrill of the Chaste* came out, I had just finished speaking at a Protestant denomination's annual conference for college journalists when an exuberant young woman presented me with a T-shirt she had designed. The brown, fitted shirt had a message on the front in small pink letters: "modest is hottest." Beneath those words, in even smaller letters, was a passage from St. Paul: "Those members of the body which we think to be less honorable, on these we bestow greater honor; and our unpresentable parts have greater modesty" (1 Cor 12:23).

I thought the shirt delightful and was eager to wear it. When I did, however, I discovered an unintended consequence. At least, I *hope* it was unintended. You see, the Bible verse was printed in such small type that people couldn't make it out unless they looked *very* closely at my, ahem, "unpresentable parts."

◆ ◆ ◆

If the "modest is hottest" crowd represents one end of the spectrum—those who seek to make modesty fashionable—on the other end, I would place the self-described "Mary-like" brigade. In writings that circulate online, they claim pious Catholic ladies are required to follow the Mother of God's own fashion rules, including ankle-length skirts, wrist-length sleeves, and a neckline that must not be more than "two fingers' breadth" from "the pit of the throat." How they are privy to such extrabiblical knowledge is a mystery. Perhaps they discovered Our Lady's fashion dos and don'ts in a trove of lost first-century scrolls, alongside other never-before-seen writings such as "What to Give the Child Who Has Everything" by the Magi and "How to Belly Dance for Your Stepfather" by Salomé.

My friend Kevin Tierney has a better way to approach the idea of Marian modesty. He says it is not just for women, and it is not just about clothes. Rather, modesty is fundamentally about being interiorly aware of your identity as a beloved son or daughter of God, made in his image; reflecting upon these things in conversation with God; and taking them into your exterior behavior. Mary is the model because St. Luke tells us that, during key events of her life (such as when the shepherds told her that angels proclaimed her child "Messiah and Lord"), she "kept all these things, reflecting on them in her heart" (Lk 2:11, 2:19). Kevin writes,

> The desire to ponder all things within the heart
> is the beginning of modesty. Just because we
> can do something does not mean we should.
> Mary could have broadcasted her thoughts on
> all these events, and nobody would blame her.
> She might even have become quite the celebrity
> for doing so. Yet then it would have been about
> her, instead of about her Son. As the Mother of
> the Redeemer, she was also His first Evangelist.
> Making things all about you and your thoughts

probably doesn't make a very good representative for a Gospel whose primary message is a willingness to cast off what is rightfully yours, live humbly and lay down your life for people who can't wait to drive nails into your flesh.[1]

In our daily life, Kevin says, this means we should "ask how much our actions look to bring attention to ourselves." For example,

When I help others, am I doing it so people can realize how generous and great I am? When I pray and sing at Mass, am I elevating my voice just a bit so everyone can hear how good I sing? Am I trying to get people to see my piety when I kneel in prayer? In short, how much am I like Christ (who lived a life of having himself despised for our sake and the honor of His Father), and how much am I like the Pharisee, who though fully and ornately clothed radiated immodesty? Once we shake off our Pharisee nature, how can we continue to grow in Christ?

Modesty must lead to something beyond ourselves. It must lead to humility.[2]

◆ ◆ ◆

When I first set chastity as a goal, my bed got the message way before my closet. My new lifestyle gave me a new kind of confidence, and I associated confidence with showing off in sexy clothes and makeup.

From adolescence and even earlier, young women are taught to use makeup and clothing as a shortcut to self-worth. They learn that with help from the makeup-counter saleswoman, they can achieve a more "mature" look that makes them stand out from their classmates. They learn that they can instantly become more popular with boys just by wearing high heels.

It's natural for girls to want to experiment with ways to dress themselves as they make the transition into womanhood. What's wrong is that our culture, through the fashion and entertainment media, tries to keep women in a girlish emotional state.

When it comes to self-image, makeup and clothing should be, at best, a crutch—good for a pick-me-up but not for a psychological foundation. Women (and men too) should be taught early on that, as Jesus said, the body—that is, our personhood—is more than clothes (Lk 12:23).

I used to see my clothing as part of a chemical formula of sorts: take me; add heavy makeup, a revealing dress, and sexy shoes; and ka-boom! Instant male reaction. Even though I knew the reaction was to my revealing clothes and not to my personality, I didn't mind because I preferred to get any reaction over none at all. I feared that if men didn't notice my body right away, I would be invisible to them. Wearing clothes and makeup that were guaranteed to get noticed, then, gave me a sense of control.

To be honest, however, there was a deeper reason I wanted control, one that I did not fully understand when I was first trying to overcome the desire to call attention to myself through clothes and makeup. The experiences of abuse I suffered in childhood (see chapter 2) had a profoundly destructive effect on my personal identity. I grew up thinking that I was valuable, not for who I was, but only for what I did.

As a teenager, believing that other people, especially men, were going to use me, I put up a false front—one that remained in place for many years, until my encounter with Christ moved me to begin to live authentically. During that time of deception, I dressed provocatively, used sexual language in everyday conversation, and sought to project an aura of sexual aggressiveness. I thought that if men were going to use me anyway, I could at least have some control over how they used me. But no matter how hard I tried to appear hardened, inside I still felt like a vulnerable, unprotected little girl.

I mention this time of my life in case you too may be tied to certain ways of dressing or acting that do not reflect your true identity as a beloved child of God. Not only women are vulnerable to the temptation to create a false self; men are too. Think of those who, trying to show how tough they are, find themselves desiring to get just "one more tattoo." If you worry that you would lose something terribly important by replacing certain modes of style with ones that show greater reverence for yourself and others, I invite you to explore the root causes of such fear. If you are seeking to expose or alter your body to compensate for interior brokenness, something is wrong. Talking to a good confessor, spiritual director, Catholic therapist, or trusted friend or family member can help.[3]

◆ ◆ ◆

Once I became chaste, my former ways of dressing were a recipe for disaster. I quickly discovered that chaste woman plus unchaste clothing equals instant hypocrite. I may have known what was in my heart, but others around me didn't. To them, I looked like a phony. It's for reasons such as this that St. Paul said to avoid all appearance of evil (see 1 Thes 5:22).

At the same time that I was unintentionally misleading others, I was fooling myself. No matter how confident I was in my chastity, the way I dressed unquestionably affected my behavior. I would conduct myself in a different way if I wore wobbly pumps and a figure-hugging outfit; it was "the iniquity of my heels" all over again.

Eventually—after some pretty awkward times trying to dress one way and act another—I realized what was the problem. I was treating chastity as if it were merely a lifestyle choice when, as with marriage, it's far more than that. It's a *vocation*, part of the "universal call to holiness."[4]

Viewing chastity as a vocation led me to want to dress in a way to suit my vocation. This was much different from the way I'd changed my wardrobe in the past, when I'd upgrade it for a new job. Now I had to rethink the way I was dressed not only at work but also every place I went. The question in my mind was no longer about how I might show my body to its best advantage, or how I might make people admire my eyes, lips, or complexion. Instead, I began to ask myself, "How am I showing people I am glad to see them? How am I seeking to brighten their day?" For I was no longer dressing for some man I hoped to attract or keep. Instead, I was dressing for everyone I would meet during the course of the day—from neighbors to coworkers, friends, family, and strangers. They have all become part of my apostolate, an apostolate of beauty.

My rules are simple. When I'm picking out an outfit, I ask myself if it makes me self-conscious about my body. Now, I don't mean, "Does it make me wish I were thinner?" I can put on just about any outfit and wish my rear end were smaller, my stomach flatter, and so on. I mean, for example, if I'm trying on a skirt, I ask myself honestly, "When people see me in this, will they be drawn to stare at my legs?" If my instincts say yes, then my instincts are probably right—it's better to find a well-styled skirt that leaves a little more to the imagination. Likewise, if I'm trying on a blouse, I ask myself, "When I walk into a room wearing this, are people's eyes going to be automatically drawn to my chest?" Again, if the answer's yes, I'm better off with a blouse that is my favorite color and fabric but not as tight or low cut.

A great thing to do is go through your closet, take out anything that doesn't fit you perfectly, and donate it to your local thrift store. There's no reason to own anything ill fitting. It's depressing, plus it leaves the uncomfortable possibility that you might try to squeeze into those too-tight jeans when everything else is in the laundry.

Many people, men and women, who believe they are overweight try to hide their bodies in clothes that are too big. If that's you, please, give the extra-large sweatshirts to the Salvation Army and spend some quality time in a store that offers fashionable clothing in larger sizes. There are so many such stores now—far more than when I was a 172-pound college student—that you shouldn't deprive yourself of the confidence that comes with dressing in a way that shows you care about how you look.

But perhaps, while not being called to wear a religious habit, you really want to avoid fashion altogether. Granted, many saints went around draped in drab, bulky, or shapeless clothes. But they were able to get away with it because they were shining with the joy of Christ. So, if you feel moved to dress plainly, be prepared to work that much harder to show others, through your words, actions, and bearing, that you love them with God's own love. With great polyester comes great responsibility.

◆ ◆ ◆

My mother has an artist's eye for clothing, finding unique and colorful pieces that reflect her creative personality. In this, she takes after her own late mother—my beloved Grandma Jessie. Grandma was so beautiful as a child that when her brothers and sisters used to reenact movies in their backyard, she always got to play the lead roles because they all loved dressing her up. I remember how much she adored accessories; as a kid, I used to play with her fancy gloves and costume jewelry.

As I set out to write this chapter, I asked my mother for her thoughts on modesty, because she herself had undergone a conversion that led her to rethink how she presented herself. She responded with a memory from Grandma's last days. It touches me to read it, because I remember how sick my grandmother was for months on end and how it seemed that nothing could make her smile. With Grandma gone, Mom's words remind me that it is such a blessing to be able to share inner and outer beauty—especially with people who don't have enough of it in their lives:

> I remember when my mom was in the hospital, dying of a dreadful disease. She could hardly move or talk. Unlike most of the hospital visitors, I did not wear jeans and a sweatshirt to see my mom. I dressed up. I was clean and sparkling, with makeup on. I looked like I was going out to a show. My mom's eyes lit up when she saw me: "You look beautiful!"
>
> Reviving my mom's spirits during those hospital visits, I realized that I was created to celebrate. In fact, I am to be a celebration for the world!

16

A THORNY ISSUE:
DEALING WITH TEMPTATION

My friend Father Augustine Wetta, O.S.B., a Texan surfer turned Benedictine monk, says that the day he entered Saint Louis Abbey as a postulant, he swore to himself that he would never again have a lustful thought. That resolution, he adds, lasted "about an hour and a half." So he decided to delay his resolution for one year, until entering the novitiate. But when his novitiate came around, he was still bothered by the same lustful thoughts. "In fact," he says, "as far as I could tell, I hadn't made any progress at all."

At that time, the then Brother Augustine had been reading a biography of St. Benedict. "I came across a passage that said when he had lustful thoughts, he used to go roll around in a rose bush. So I said to myself, 'That's easy. If St. Benedict can do it, then so can I.' And I went out into the garden behind the monastery and jumped into one of our rose bushes."

Did it work? Not in the way the young novice intended.

"To make a long story short, I got stuck in that rose bush and spent a very uncomfortable hour and a half trying to get out—then another awkward twenty minutes or so trying to explain myself to the monk that found me there."

Thankfully, Father Augustine's novice master had a sense of humor. "Once he finished laughing at me, he explained I had failed to take into account three important differences between St. Benedict and me: first, that St. Benedict jumped into a *wild* rose bush, which has considerably smaller thorns than the cultivated variety; second, that St. Benedict was naked when he did it, so he didn't get his clothes caught up in the thorns; and third, that *he* was a saint." The moral of the story? "Rolling around in a rose bush might be a good thing for a saint to do," Father Augustine allows, "but for the rest of us, it's kind of stupid."

◆ ◆ ◆

I love Father Augustine's story, because it captures how I felt when I first began to get serious about chastity. At the same time, it leaves me with a question: If I can't fight temptation by imitating the saints, how *can* I fight temptation?

Stephen Beale, a journalist and convert to Catholic faith from Evangelical Protestantism, has a different perspective than Father Augustine. He writes in a column about Benedict and the rosebush, as well as about an episode from the life of St. Thomas Aquinas involving a similarly violent reaction to sexual thoughts, and comes to a very interesting conclusion. But first, it will help to have some background on Aquinas.

Thomas came from a noble Italian family that, recognizing his religious vocation, had planned from his childhood for him to live comfortably at a well-funded Benedictine monastery. When, as a teenager studying at the University of Naples, Thomas ran off to join the newly formed Dominican Order, whose members supported themselves by begging, his mother was scandalized. Unable to convince her son to return home, she decided to take drastic action.

Thomas's mother had two of his brothers kidnap him, imprisoning him in a room in one of the family's castles. There, one by one, members of the family harangued the friar, trying to talk him out of his Dominican vocation. When it became clear that this strategy wasn't working, two of Thomas's brothers decided to try another, more sinister tack. Hoping to tempt him to break his vow of chastity, they hired a prostitute and shoved her into his room. What happened next has become the stuff of legend. Thomas grabbed a flaming piece of wood from the fireplace and brandished it at the woman, chasing her out of the room.

In *My Peace I Give You*, I talk about how this story, which I believe is true, has been misrepresented over the years by people, including the otherwise excellent G. K. Chesterton, who treat it as farce. I don't think it was funny for Thomas to have his family members—the very people who should have been protecting him—conspire to assault his purity.

Stephen Beale, the columnist, likewise doesn't find Thomas's plight a laughing matter. Reflecting on Thomas's chasing the prostitute and Benedict's jumping into the rosebush, he says, "Both stories are compelling because of the profound simplicity with which each saint confronted sexual temptation. The response of each saint was direct and immediate—and, in both cases, neither one spent much time hand wringing over how awful it was that they were sensing sexual temptation in the first place. Both saints instead show how, sometimes, it pays to respond physically to a physical problem."[1] Beale makes a profound point about how some of the seemingly extreme practices of the saints can have relevance for our real and often messy lives.

Over the years since making chastity a priority, I have reached a point where I am not troubled by sexual temptation as often or as strongly as in the past. But I still have to be watchful, and occasionally I am blindsided by feelings of attraction that can take me back to a state of discomfort that I had hoped was long in my past.

Such discomfort does not come from simple frustration. If it were only that, I could resolve it easily enough by finding a healthy means of distraction. However, it usually has its root in something deeper: an emotional memory that has affected me so profoundly that it has taken on a physical component. Depending upon the personality of the man who triggers it, it may be a traumatic memory, such as the pain of having been abused, or the sadness of having been rejected.

I suspect that for many who have suffered from the misuse of sex—whether abuse, or their own sexual sins— memories of loss, fear, or anger can trigger a sense of emptiness that seems all-encompassing. It is the emptiness of a person who is not comfortable in his or her own skin: the emptiness of a person who is *wounded*. In this emptiness, the possibility of being desired by the object of one's attraction can appear as a way to feel like something rather than nothing.

That is why, even though I agree with Father Augustine that, for many of us, rolling around in a rosebush might be "kind of stupid," it is not at all stupid to follow Beale's advice and do as the saints have done: "respond physically to a physical problem."

For good reason, St. Matthew records twice that Jesus said, "If your right eye offends you, pluck it out" (Mt 5:29, 18:9). In identifying lust as a physical phenomenon, rather than merely a state of mind, Jesus wasn't just speaking to the weak or spiritually immature. He was speaking to all of us.

Concupiscence—the inclination to sin—isn't washed away by Baptism any more than are other physical frailties (CCC 1266). It is not something that can be overcome just by thinking enlightened thoughts about the goodness and beauty of the human body. Pope Francis observes, "It is very hard to cut ties with a sinful situation. It is hard! . . . But the voice of God tells us this word: Flee! You cannot fight here, because the fire, the sulfur will kill you. Flee!"[2] In the battle against temptation, fleeing is not cowardly. It is *courageous*.

◆ ◆ ◆

The idea that intellectual virtue is the same as moral virtue is known as the "Socratic error." Socrates—or at least Plato's conception of him—claimed that the soul alone was what made a human, human. Against the Socratic error, the Church defends the goodness of the human body, recognizing that the body is essential to our identity: "Spirit and matter, in man, are not two natures united, but rather their union forms a single nature" (CCC 365).

When body and soul are understood as a unity, it is clear that virtue cannot be merely intellectual. Prayer is certainly essential in overcoming the temptation to lust, and other, healthy mental distractions can help, like conversing with a friend who supports you in your chastity, or doing spiritual reading. A successful effort, however, will be multifaceted, involving your entire, embodied person.

What such an effort looks like will be different for each individual. It may be as simple as averting your gaze from someone whose appearance excites you. Or it may be taking up a form of exercise that releases pent-up tension without requiring you to be around body-conscious gym members—such as walking, biking, or gardening. Come to think of it, perhaps rosebushes aren't such a bad idea for fighting lust—trimming them, that is, not rolling in them.

◆ ◆ ◆

I am part of the last generation of American public school students that was not taught at a young age that masturbation is healthy and normal. Today, the US government promotes teaching kindergartners about touching their genitals to "feel good," and, as I write, efforts are underway in the United Nations to require such "education" for children from age newborn to four. I say this not out of a desire to shock but simply to acknowledge that, if you went to public schools, it is very likely that you have been subject to government-led efforts to convince you that the Church is wrong when it says masturbation is "an intrinsically and gravely disordered action" (CCC 2352).

But it is not only the government that is trying to tell you masturbation is good. The entire culture is also doing so through film, television, print media, and, most especially, electronic media such as the Internet. In this area too things have changed since I was a child. I can remember when a person who sought pornography had to leave his or her home to find it or order it delivered by regular mail to his home. Today, pornography to suit every perverted desire known to humans, including exploitation of children and enslaved adults, is available to all with a tap on a computer or phone.

If you suffer the temptation to masturbate or to view pornography, or if someone close to you does, there are good Catholic resources available that can help bring healing. I especially recommend Arlington Diocese Bishop Paul S. Loverde's pastoral letter on purity, "Bought with a Price," and its associated website, which was developed in consultation with experts in the field of sex addiction.[3] To what Loverde has said, I can add only a personal thought. But perhaps it can help.

The Church teaches that masturbation is wrong not because the Church hates sex (have you looked at the size of some observant Catholic families lately?). Rather, masturbation is wrong because it seeks sexual pleasure apart from a *relationship*, namely, marriage, "in which the total meaning of mutual self-giving and human procreation in the context of true love is achieved" (CCC 2352). So masturbation is a sin against God in part because it is a sin against *union*, a union that is especially important because it represents the union of Christ and his Church (Eph 5:25, 32).

When I learned that the Church teaches that masturbation is effectively a sin against *union*, it resonated with my own experience. I was not raised with any kind of guilt, Catholic or otherwise, about masturbation. During the time before I sought to live chastely, there was no reason I should have felt uncomfortable about it. Yet I always associated it with a kind of despair. It was, at best, a willful self-medication against the pain of loneliness, and it always came with a cost. The cost was having to repress the ever-deepening awareness that all the physical pleasure in the world could not compensate for the absence of someone who would love me for who I was.

At the time I was writing the original edition of this book, and for a short time thereafter, I followed the writings of various authors who called themselves "feminist," "sex positive," "pro-choice," and so on. They were antagonistic against the Church, and they seemed never to tire of mocking people who promoted sexual abstinence outside of marriage.

It seemed to me when I was following these writers, and it seems to me now, that the entire enterprise of promoting sexual "liberation" requires the same sort of emotional and spiritual repression that I suffered when I was trying to self-medicate with physical pleasure. I mention this, not to judge the hearts of those who antagonize the Church—they honestly may not know what they do—but to suggest that what some people call "natural" is not necessarily authentic.

That which is most truly natural in us finds its fulfillment through obeying the natural law, a law established by reason in the heart of every human being. Obeying the natural law in this fallen world is hard; it requires the help of grace. But, while such obedience may not bring us immediate pleasure, if we follow the natural law where it leads—toward the Creator who satisfies all desire—it will bring us joy, a joy we can begin to taste even in this life. We violate it at our own peril.

◆ ◆ ◆

Besides the Benedictine priest I mentioned, there is another Augustine who has something helpful to say about fighting the temptation to lust. The *Catechism* quotes a prayer from St. Augustine's *Confessions* in which the saint recalls having a mistaken understanding of continence (the virtue of sexual restraint): "I thought that continence arose from one's own powers, which I did not recognize in myself. I was foolish enough not to know . . . that no one can be continent unless you grant it. For you would surely have granted it if my inner groaning had reached your ears and I with firm faith had cast my cares on you" (CCC 2520). You can see in that short passage why Augustine is called the Doctor of Grace. Part of his contribution to Christian thought was reminding the faithful that, when God crowns their merits, he is crowning his own gifts.[4]

A confessor helped me understand this ancient truth upon hearing me confess having lustful thoughts. I told him I had tried to resist them, "but didn't try hard enough."

The priest gently pointed out to me that, although I was right to resist such thoughts, in a certain sense I had the wrong attitude. I was acting as though each battle against lust was mine to fight alone. A better way, he said, would be not to wait until the temptation was over before speaking to God. Rather, I should admit to God, "I can't deal with this temptation. I need *you* to deal with it."

In practice, I have found that taking such a tack does not mean giving up the fight. It means taking the fight to the next level: learning what it means to say with St. Paul that "I can do all things in him who strengthens me" (Phil 4:13 RSV). And it means following St. Benedict's advice, in the prologue of his Rule, to take tempting thoughts, while they are yet weak, and dash them against the rock that is Christ. That is the only way to emerge from temptation smelling like a rose.

17

WINNING THE SPIRITUAL BATTLE

When I was in high school, a friend who collected vinyl LP records introduced me to a vintage album by a rock band lampooning the "if it feels good, do it" philosophy of the late 1960s, a philosophy that still prevails today. The band was the Mothers of Invention, led by Frank Zappa; the album was *We're Only in It for the Money*; and the best track on it asked the musical question, "What's the ugliest part of your body?" The answer: "your mind."

Chastity is, first and foremost, a mental discipline. You can try to push yourself by displaying self-control when your heart isn't in it, but keeping it up over the long haul requires dedication.

Because the foundation of your chastity is within you, the greatest challenges to it lurk within as well. Some of these challenges you may know all too well. They are the temptations that you have to put out of your mind—such as when an acquaintance with a reputation for quickly disposing of romantic partners suggests he or she would like to get to know you better. They also include the feelings of loneliness and uncertainty, such as when you spend the night home alone after politely declining the acquaintance's invitation. But that is not what I have in mind just now. It is the time when you feel most confident in your ability to resist temptation, and when you feel least susceptible to loneliness, that you have to be on your guard for what is spiritually the most dangerous challenge to chastity: the unexpected, utterly embarrassing, seemingly irrational obsession.

By nature, an obsession comes about when you least expect it. You may be putting your resources into projecting confidence and self-control, repressing the vulnerable child inside you that fears rejection. But that vulnerable child still dwells in you—and is still fascinated by the potential spouse who seems unattainable.

Normally, it is possible to work your way through an obsession without much trouble. It takes prayer, determination, and maintaining focus on your goal. On rare occasions, however, the obsession may succeed in burying its hooks deeply into your psyche—something I once learned the hard way.

◆ ◆ ◆

In the spring of 2004, I was living chastely but not particularly hopefully. I felt bored and complacent. None of the men I knew were romantic possibilities. I had recently turned down some invitations from men who were clearly not interested in waiting for wedding vows, and I was feeling confident of my ability to hold out for marriage—more confident than I'd ever been before. Too confident.

Ian (not his real name) was a man at my workplace whom I had known casually before beginning my job, as we traveled in the same circles. Besides thinking him handsome, I admired him for various qualities—he was debonair, intelligent, and well spoken—but he never seemed to notice me. He would walk by my desk every day but never say hello, even though we had chatted a few times among mutual friends.

One day, a coworker I barely knew was leaving for another job, and my office took the opportunity to hold a send-off for him at a nearby bar. It seemed like ages since I'd been to a party, so I brought a flashy, above-the-knee dress to work that day and changed into it before going to the send-off. (I had yet to work out the wardrobe aspect of chastity.) Ian was there, scotch and soda in hand, and to my surprise, he struck up a conversation with me—complimenting me on my dress.

I am never so vulnerable as when a man I admire pays me an unexpected compliment. As a sense of lightheadedness set in, I stayed by Ian's side for more than an hour, and he didn't seem to mind.

Ian, it transpired, *really* liked his liquor. Unconsciously, I found myself returning to the mindset I had when I used to hang around rock musicians after concerts: I figured that if I stuck around long enough, they would get drunk enough to want to spend the rest of the night with me.

Needless to say, by slipping back into the familiar role of enabler, I was going completely against my better judgment. My true desire was not for a man who drank to get drunk, let alone one who wouldn't want me unless he'd had a few. But I was drunk—not with alcohol but with excitement that *Ian noticed me*.

He wound up walking me the fifteen blocks downtown to where I would catch my train home. On the way, he confessed that he was lonely and suffered from depression. I sighed inwardly—not with genuine sympathy for Ian's pain but with thoughts of how it might work to my advantage. *He's so vulnerable. How sweet. He must really like me, to be opening up like this.* I told him that I used to suffer from depression myself, until I came to faith. Did he have faith? He didn't but wished he had. In my mind, I was already imagining myself as being the girlfriend who would help him see the light.

If I allowed my better judgment to take hold, I would have known I was fooling myself. I can't stop a man from drinking too much coffee, let alone make one stop drinking alcohol, stop being depressed, and get down on his knees to make an Act of Contrition. Granted, to enter into marriage, a man and woman must commit to bearing with each other's infirmities. However, I don't believe it is a great idea to choose for one's spouse a "handyman's special."

Before I knew it, Ian and I were at the train station. He gave me a confused look—as though he wasn't sure whether or how he should kiss me good-bye. Then he leaned down—he was tall—to give me a lightning-fast kiss on the lips, and he was off. I thought about Ian all the way home and went to bed with fantasies of him. In the morning, I awoke with a mixture of hope and fear—and still, I couldn't stop thinking about him.

The hope was short-lived. Very quickly, it became clear that what I had taken as interest from Ian was really just curiosity—and that curiosity had been satisfied. He might like to occasionally have a drink with me and share his troubles, but that would be it.

Normally, upon realizing that my love interest had lost interest, I would pick myself up and move on. For reasons I didn't understand, that didn't happen. Instead, I started regressing back to the kind of mentality I had in high school, when I feared that losing a potential boyfriend meant losing my last chance for love.

One night, since a mutual friend had invited Ian and me to a party, we met up beforehand and arrived there together. Upon our arrival, Ian proceeded to work the room as if I weren't there. I remember feeling personally injured by the slight—too enmeshed in my fantasy world to realize he and I weren't really on a date. I didn't want to be confused by the facts.

Coming at a point when my romantic life was so uneventful compared to former times, congratulating myself on being so godly and chaste, this obsessive attraction blindsided me. Worst of all, I had to deal with it in the workplace. I used to tolerate Ian's walking by without saying hello. Now, whenever he seemed to ignore me, I was crushed.

I sought to regain control of the situation—but not the way I should have, by controlling myself. Instead, my workplace outfits became progressively more revealing. I would pop into Ian's office on some slim pretext, looking for a bit of conversation, but I was so nervous that I'd only wind up embarrassing myself.

After a couple of weeks of being unable to get Ian out of my mind, it started to dawn on me that I had a problem. Although I was extremely reluctant to give up my hope that he might someday fall in love with me, it was clear that I couldn't continue to have him at the center of my thoughts. I was having trouble sleeping and was often on the verge of tears. Really, I feared I was going crazy. The worst part was that I knew on some level that my obsession wasn't rational, yet it seemed there was nothing I could do about it. I felt helpless and didn't understand why.

Finally, I called my mother and asked for help. She listened as I told her about how I had fallen into a crush that felt terribly wrong. Even if Ian were right for me and liked me back, I explained, it was clear that my feelings for him weren't the way they were supposed to be. Love, I knew, could make one a bit silly or uncomfortable—but not physically ill and borderline insane.

Taking my complaint very seriously, Mom advised me to read up on spiritual warfare—especially Paul's words in 2 Corinthians, where he distinguishes between physical enemies and spiritual enemies: "For, although we are in the flesh, we do not battle according to the flesh, for the weapons of our battle are not of flesh but are enormously powerful, capable of destroying fortresses. We destroy arguments and every pretension raising itself against the knowledge of God, and take every thought captive in obedience to Christ" (2 Cor 10:3–5). To take every thought captive means being the master of one's thoughts and passions instead of being mastered by them. It made sense to me; that was what I needed to do. I needed spiritual help, because I was locked, however unwillingly, in a spiritual battle.

The solution, Paul advised, is to "[put] on the armor of God" (Eph 6:13)—which, like the weapons of the enemy, are spiritual, not physical. Far from imaginary protection, this spiritual armor is a set of real inner qualities that are recognized for their power to shield one from spiritual harm: truth, righteousness, preparedness, faith, salvation, and prayer.

With Paul's words in mind, I began a two-pronged counterattack. I prayed each day for God to cover me with spiritual armor, and at the same time, I opened up to a few of my closest friends and family members, asking them to pray that I be released from my obsession.

Immediately upon beginning the counterattack, my symptoms began to ease. The choked-up feeling dissipated, as did much of my nervousness around Ian. I asked more friends to pray for me. It was embarrassing to admit what I was going through, but they understood. These were close friends, mind you, not ones who would gossip.

The more that people were supporting my own prayers with theirs, the more peace I began to feel and the better able I was to don my spiritual armor. Within a week, I was back to normal. It was much longer before I could be comfortable around Ian, but at least I could practice self-control, no longer pining for him or pursuing him.

◆ ◆ ◆

As the saying goes, the price of liberty is eternal vigilance. Chastity is true liberty: freedom from slavery to passions that are damaging or counterproductive. It is also freedom to experience passions—but by choice, under the governance of reason, and not by the compulsion that comes when harmful habits have their way. What I learned from my experience with obsession is that I can't take that freedom for granted. The moment you allow chinks in your spiritual armor, the spirit of darkness will seep in like a lethal gas.

That "two-pronged counterattack" of personal prayer and outside prayer support I mentioned remains as vital to me in spiritual warfare today as it was in 2004—only now, as a Catholic, I have the advantage of many more prongs.

The most vital weapons in spiritual warfare are participation in the sacraments—especially regular confession and frequent Mass (daily, if you can)—and the Rosary. Even if you have only venial sins to confess,[1] regular confession will bring fruit; as the *Catechism* says, it "helps us form our conscience, fight against evil tendencies, let ourselves be healed by Christ and progress in the life of the Spirit" (*CCC* 1458).

If the idea of going to daily Mass sounds dull, perhaps you are not putting enough into it. A good book on praying the Mass can help; my favorite is Fulton J. Sheen's classic *Calvary and the Mass* (reprinted by Alba House, 2010). Remember, it is not so important that you "feel" what is happening at the eucharistic liturgy. Grace is invisible and intangible, and many of the greatest saints have had years of their lives when they did not "feel" anything upon receiving the Eucharist. What is essential is that you believe that Jesus, in the Mass, makes himself really present in the Eucharist through the liturgical words and actions of the priest. When you understand what is happening on the altar—that you are spiritually offering your own very self to be transformed in Christ—it is impossible not to be spiritually strengthened as you assist with your heart, mind, and voice.

As for the Rosary, the important thing to know is that its power, as with all sacramentals,[2] lies not in its words alone but in how much you personally enter into the mysteries as you pray them. It is especially helpful for healing the imagination. If you are not familiar with the Rosary, or would like some new inspirations, the Knights of Columbus have the excellent *Scriptural Rosary for Peace and for the Family*, available online as a free download.[3]

There are many other sacramentals and other weapons of spiritual warfare, and it would take another book to tell about them all. (The best book on the topic, in my opinion, isn't actually marketed as a work about spiritual combat, but that is what it is: *Peace of Soul*, another gem by Fulton J. Sheen [reprinted by Liguori/Triumph in 1996]). But I would say that, apart from the Rosary, the sacramental that has helped me the most is my membership in the Angelic Warfare Confraternity (www.angelicwarfare.org), an official apostolate of the Dominican Order. The confraternity is, in the words of its website, "a supernatural fellowship of men and women bound to one another in love and dedicated to pursuing and promoting chastity together under the powerful patronage of St. Thomas Aquinas and the Blessed Virgin Mary." Being a member plugs you into a kind of "prayer pipeline," joining you spiritually not only to fellow members but also with the entire Dominican Order, so that you benefit from all the order's prayers, and they from yours.

◆ ◆ ◆

Praying for our heart's desire according to God's will is how we align ourselves with our purpose in life. When we make our plans without consulting God, we are like trains with faulty wheels that keep threatening to spin off the track. Something as simple as a heartfelt prayer can send us back in the direction we are supposed to be going.

At the time of the first edition of this book, I commuted to my job at the New York *Daily News* via an underground train called the PATH (Port Authority Trans Hudson). My habit was to take a seat all the way up front by the driver's compartment, where I could see the signals. When I wasn't burying my nose in a book for the thirteen-minute ride, I would think about what those signals meant.

As long as the driver is on the right track, he knows where his destination is, but he can't see it while he's in the long, dark tunnel. All he can see are these little lights that blink red, green, or yellow. To me, that is like the life of one who is following God. Even when I know my goal is holiness, I still have to watch that I don't rush into things when God wants me to go slow, or stay in one place when he wants me to press on.

Once, when I had a moment to chat with the driver before the train started, I asked him, "How many signals are there between here and New York?"

"Oh, I don't know—forty, fifty," he replied.

"And you have to watch for every one," I marveled. "I really admire how you can do that—all the concentration it takes, because any one of those signals could turn into a red light."

I wasn't being sarcastic, and I don't think he took it that way. Still, he told me, in the nicest way possible, that my romanticism was ludicrous.

"It's a *boring* job," he said.

My face fell.

"It's the same thing every day. It's boring," he repeated. "I'm stuck here in this vertical coffin, on this metal seat . . ."

He went on. I tried to look sympathetic. In another moment, I was saved by the bell signifying the closing train doors.

I realized that when the PATH train driver leaves his "vertical coffin," he may think he is finished watching signals for the day. His job is hard, but his life is relatively easy.

With me, it is the opposite. I love watching the train signals because they are so clear. It is when I leave the train that I worry, because God's signals become obscured by the distractions of everyday life. So, I still envy the driver for the certainty he has by way of those flashing lights. And I am thankful for every day that God's Word gives me light on my "PATH."

18

WHY SHARED VALUES MATTER

My mother likes to talk about something I said one time when I was about ten or so and she asked me what was the most important quality I would look for in a boyfriend. (At the time, it was most definitely a hypothetical question, though I admit that when I was six, I was briefly "married" to my classmate Greg Clayton.)

I answered, "That he likes me."

Ah, if it were only that simple, right? My response reflected a feeling deep inside that influenced my decisions throughout my dating life, until I began to live the life of faith. I overestimated the value of a man's desire to commit to me—and underestimated my own desirability. It was a kind of superstition that affected the way I entered relationships, making me vulnerable to men who wanted an instant commitment.

First of all, any man I found appealing had the surprise factor going for him if he wanted to be in a relationship with me. It always stunned me when someone I liked returned my interest. So, I would enter into a committed relationship before I knew what I was getting into. In such a situation, there would inevitably come a time when I would realize that my boyfriend and I disagreed about things that were important to me. Unfortunately—and this is where my superstition came up—I would often try to gloss over the differences, reasoning that the mere fact that "he liked me" should be sufficient to cover everything.

What I didn't understand then, and am beginning to understand now, is this: the only way that a man and a woman in a relationship can work out their biggest and most troublesome differences over time is if they are in love. A man and a woman can be in love only if they each love what is in the other. If a man does not love the most fundamental truth of my existence—the faith underlying the values that help make me who I am—then, while he may feel a *kind* of love toward me, he doesn't really love me.

With real love, you are defined by who and what you love, rather than by who loves you. Because I have come to know and believe that God is love, I believe that in a truly loving relationship, both the man and the woman love God, and so they become God's love to each other.

In looking to God, we become like him: "We all, . . . beholding the glory of the Lord, are being changed into his likeness from one degree of glory to another" (2 Cor 3:18 RSV). It is a kind of spiritual osmosis, an almost chemical reaction from being near the source of love—and, as with a chemical reaction, it affects every part of our being. Through it, we are renewed and we learn how to love more deeply.

So, what is the difference between the love of a someone who loves you without knowing or loving God, and that of one who knows the true source of his or her love? It is like the difference between a canal and a river.

I recently took a walk along the Delaware and Raritan Canal in southern New Jersey near the Pennsylvania border. It is a lovely body of water, still and calm, and surrounded by graceful trees and foliage. One could be content to linger there for a while—if one didn't know what lay beyond. But I wasn't satisfied, because I knew there was something more just around the bend. I followed the canal until it finally opened up into its source: the Delaware River. Wham! Suddenly I had gone from a place of stillness and quiet to a grand, rushing river. Here, too, was nature—but in far greater diversity, with more kinds of flowers, trees, birds, animals, and insects. At some points, the river was bordered by rocks; at others, hanging willows. The river's rushing ripples were far more exciting than the canal's placid stillness. Yet, if I wanted, by watching their repetitive motion for a time, I could fall into their rhythms and enjoy a feeling of relaxation.

The love that is joined only to its object is the canal. The love that is joined first to a greater source and then—through that source, to its object—is the river.

◆ ◆ ◆

I met Todd in the summer of 2002, when I was between two worlds.[1] It was after I had become a Christian but before I had begun to really walk the walk (let alone consider walking all the way into the Catholic Church).

We met at a barbecue at a friend's house and hit it off right away. At thirty-two, he was a year younger than me. I liked how he seemed gentlemanly and civilized—not like the musicians and writers I was used to being with. He also had a great sense of humor, and he knew so much about such a wide range of subjects—from Greek philosophy to American history and British science-fiction films—that I felt I wouldn't be bored around him.

We wound up going to a movie together that very night. I knew I was in for a good time from the chivalrous way Todd offered to carry my popcorn. Afterward, we repaired to a cozy café and talked about our belief systems.

I told him about the faith experience I'd had a few years earlier that had changed me from an agnostic Jew to a Bible-believing Christian. He told me he was a devout atheist—and he wanted to kiss me.

Although I was not yet set on chastity, my old way of life was getting tired. After one kiss, I confessed to Todd that I didn't kiss just to fool around anymore; a relationship was what I was after. He said he wasn't interested in just fooling around either; it wasn't in his nature. He said it quite seriously, and although part of me felt like the most gullible woman on earth, I believed him.

It turned out that he was indeed telling the truth. In fact, as I got to know him, I learned that he was incapable of telling a lie. In the words of Bob Dylan, "To live outside the law, you must be honest." I was to learn that for a devout atheist such as Todd, intent on proving he could live within society but outside divine law, ethics were essential to survival.

◆ ◆ ◆

From the start, Todd had many qualities that I had dreamed of finding in a boyfriend. He was devoted and faithful, and he enjoyed introducing me to his numerous friends. It had been so long since I had been treated like a girlfriend and not just a pal or lover, and I relished the feeling.

At first, we got around our religious differences by playing the "live and let live" game. I could keep my prayers to myself, and Todd could try not to say anything about how all religious faith was based on superstition. That last part was very hard for him, for he was not merely an atheist but a proudly *dogmatic* atheist—a lifetime subscriber to the *Skeptical Inquirer* ("The Magazine for Science and Reason").

Not surprisingly, we weren't able to live and let live for long. Even before our truce inevitably evaporated into bickering over the Bible, something didn't feel right. I began to notice that although Todd was unusually kind and loyal to his friends, he didn't seem to particularly care about anyone else. He was polite to all, but struck me as being very much in his own world. As far as I could tell, the closest he got to voicing concern over strangers was when he would discuss politics. Even then, he seemed more concerned about dangers to large economic entities than dangers to individuals.

I felt that something was missing from my relationship with Todd, but I didn't know what it was. One day, in an effort to fill the gap, I asked Todd if he would consider volunteering with me. A friend of mine volunteered for a charity that delivered hot meals to elderly shut-ins on Saturday mornings; maybe she, Todd, and I could do it together. Todd responded with a lengthy lecture. The gist of it was that the capitalist system works by enabling citizens to choose how to use their time; he did not choose to use his time volunteering, and therefore other citizens were free to volunteer in his place. He also stated that while he was personally opposed to donating his time, he gave society other intangible benefits by writing articles that supported the capitalist system.

My mind got a bit muddled trying to reconcile this seemingly heartless Scrooge with the sweet, gentle man who was always there for his friends. Hoping to find some corner of his heart that was open to faith, I started to share with him about how God had healed my depression. Todd responded my testimony as one would humor a child telling about the tooth fairy. He was willing to believe that I'd been depressed, and that I was now better, but he insisted God had nothing to do with it. Whatever change had taken place was purely psychological—the result of my own gullibility and positive thinking, he said.

The more Todd denied that God was responsible for what I believed were the fruits of my faith, the more distant

I felt from him. I tried to explain to him what was wrong, but it seemed there was no way I could make him understand. To him, I was just being unreasonable. He insisted he loved me, and he made every effort he could to satisfy me—short of changing his beliefs.

◆ ◆ ◆

To better convey what transpired between Todd and me, and what it says about the importance of shared values, I offer an allegory. As with many of my favorite allegories, this one involves fattening food:

JUST DESSERTS

One beautiful morning, I woke up and found a tray full of unbaked cookies on my windowsill, all perfectly formed and ready to be baked. As I looked at the tray in amazement, I heard a beautiful voice in my head—the voice of a perfect Being. It said, "I love you, I care about you, and I will give you a tray of cookies every morning for the rest of your life. All you have to do is bake them."

I wondered if I was going crazy, but I baked the cookies anyway and tried them. They were delicious—so much better than anything I could have created myself. I had to share them with everyone I knew—and I did. My life started to change. I never before felt as though I had so much to give. I could share all the cookies I had, and they would always be replenished in the morning. For once, I felt I had a purpose.

When I met Todd, the first thing I did was offer him one of my cookies. He was enthralled and had to have more. So, I gave Todd more cookies—and told him of how they appeared on my windowsill every morning, given to me by Someone I couldn't see who loved me very much. My only contribution was putting them in the oven and taking them out in time.

"That's impossible," Todd said. He had sometimes noticed my taking a tray of batter from my windowsill but assumed it was some odd baker's trick of leaving the dough out overnight. In any case, he wasn't interested enough in my cookies' origin to do the research necessary to discover where they came from.

"How can it be impossible?" I asked. "Where else would the cookies come from? I never used to get them before."

He had heard about such things, he said. In every case, the origin of the mysterious cookies turned out to be a figment of the baker's imagination.

"What are you talking about?" I exclaimed. "You tasted them. They're real."

"Yes," he said, "the cookies themselves are real, but they didn't come from some imaginary being. You made them."

"But I told you I found them!" I protested. "Are you calling me a liar?"

"No."

"Then you're calling me crazy?"

"No, not at all. You're making the cookies unconsciously. There is a known psychological condition by which an otherwise sane person has a mental block, so that she forgets the time she spends each day making cookies."

"Now, that's crazy," I said. "Think about it: What's more probable, that I'm getting the cookie dough from Someone else or that my otherwise sane mind is completely erasing the fact that I'm making it myself?"

We argued for a while longer, with Todd using my personal weaknesses to score points. He observed that some mornings I didn't bake cookies at all, and some mornings I burned the cookies and they were no good. In both instances, it was through my own fault or neglect—there was nothing wrong with the dough I had been given. However, he took my not baking them perfectly every day as evidence that they came from me—and not from a perfect Being. After all, he reasoned, if a perfect Being made them, they would always be perfect.

Exasperated, I left off arguing for a while. Todd tried to make me feel better—baking me some cookies of his own. Most of them he kept for himself, though he was generous to me and others in his inner circle.

As Todd and I tried to patch things up, I suggested an experiment. It would mean a lot to me, I said, if we would share the experience of baking cookies together. And so, one morning, the two of us gathered in the kitchen—me with my ready-made dough from the windowsill and him with his own batter recipe. We tried to combine the two, expecting an amazing new flavor sensation.

It was not to be. My dough and his refused to mix. They had different densities, and no matter how much we needed—I mean, kneaded— them together, they always separated.

There's more to the story, but I'll leave off there.

My dough is my natural gifts elevated by God's grace, or rather, graces. To each person who lives by faith, unique graces become manifest every day: "His mercies . . . are new every morning" (Lam 3:22–23 RSV). The act of baking represents my works—what I do with the graces I have been given. I can choose whether to cooperate with grace and give of my resources, and how to do so.

Todd's dough is his natural gifts—period. His baking cookies from his own dough is his determined attempt to do good works without cooperating with grace. Hence, when his dough meets mine, it can't mix, because it positively *resists* mixing—like oil encountering water.

The problem is not that Todd can't do any good works without God. He can. The problem is that ultimately it is not enough to do good. We are called to *be* good—sharing in God's very life.[2] This life is the life of grace in which we begin to partake with our Baptism; it is strengthened by our participation in the Eucharist, confession, and other sacraments, and is fulfilled with the divinization that awaits us in heaven. Christ's Transfiguration points to this divinization, which he promises to those who remain in him to the end. That is what the Church means when it says, "our participation in the Eucharist already gives us a foretaste of Christ's transfiguration of our bodies" (CCC 1000).

Since I was not yet Catholic, I did not know all these things when, after seven months of dating, I finally broke up with Todd. What I did know was that, however true his feelings were for me from his perspective, he could not love me in the truest sense, for he could not love me in Christ. Later I would find a similar understanding expressed by Augustine as he says to God in his *Confessions*: "There is no true friendship unless You weld it between souls that cleave together through that charity which is shed in our hearts by the Holy Ghost who is given to us."[3]

◆ ◆ ◆

Years later, as a Catholic, I learned that another Protestant woman who made the decision to become Catholic made a like decision to leave her atheist lover—but, in her case, the breakup was much more painful.

"It is terribly hard to even mention my religious feelings to you," she wrote to her lover in a letter, "because I am sure you do not think I am sincere. But it is not a sudden thing, but a thing which has been growing in me for years.

I had impulses toward religion again and again and now when I try to order my life according to it in order to attain some sort of peace and happiness it is very hard but I must do it. Because even though it is hard, it gives me far more happiness to do it, even though it means my combating my physical feelings toward you."[4]

The woman who wrote those words was thirty-year-old Dorothy Day, who (as I mentioned in chapter 8) may well be named a saint one day. She was writing in 1928 to her longtime live-in partner Forster Batterham, the father of her infant daughter and a radical so opposed to societal mores that he refused to solemnize their relationship with vows.

Although her letters to Batterham would not see print until after her death in 1980, Day's 1952 autobiography, *The Long Loneliness*, offers a poignant glimpse of how her conversion cost her Forster's companionship. She writes, "We loved each other so strongly that he wanted me to remain in the love of the moment; he wanted me to rest in that love. He cried out against my attitude that there would be nothing left of that love without a faith."[5]

Day's friends, who knew her before her conversion when she was a radical activist, whispered that she was drawn to Catholicism because she was sick of sex. That was not her perspective. As she tells it, she did not turn to God in order to shut sex out. Rather, she so loved her family life with Forster and their daughter so much that she only wanted to let divine love in. "[Through] a whole love, both physical and spiritual, I came to know God."[6] It was only Batterham's refusal to walk with her—to respect her faith even just enough to marry her and permit her to raise their daughter Catholic—that led her to choose God over the great love of her life.

That choice ultimately led Day to found (with her mentor Peter Maurin) the Catholic Worker, a movement that would inspire many thousands of people to perform works of mercy toward those in need. She lived chastely, never marrying, and there was a time early on when she questioned whether her efforts to build the movement were worth forgoing family life. But then she writes, "I thought indignantly—'But I *am* a woman of family. I have had husband and home life—I have a daughter. . . . How can I let anybody put over on me the idea that I am a single person? I am a mother, and the mother of a very large family at that.'"[7]

I look at Dorothy Day's life, and I see true spiritual motherhood. She was deeply human and knew "the long loneliness." But she also knew that her deepest loneliness was not for mere companionship. It was for companionship in Christ. As she wrote in her autobiography, Day found that companionship through an intimate relationship with Jesus in the Eucharist, through weekly confession, and through giving others the love she herself had received: "We cannot love God unless we love each other, and to love we must know each other. We know him in the breaking of bread, and we know each other in the breaking of bread, and we are not alone anymore."[8]

1 9

BELIEVING IS SEEING

For a few months when I was between jobs, I did medical billing for my stepfather, an optometrist who specializes in low-vision patients. I learned something there: people who are losing their eyesight are not a particularly happy bunch.

My stepfather is, by contrast, one of the most relentlessly upbeat people I have ever met. He refuses to give up on cases that other doctors deem hopeless, and he exhorts his patients not to give up on themselves.

Working in my stepfather's office and watching how his patients responded to his encouragement, I saw that those who got the most out of treatment were the ones who were the most hopeful, no matter how bleak their prognosis. Those who came in with dark clouds over their heads were unlikely to improve much, no matter what my stepfather tried to do for them. Those who got better were the ones who had hope—if not in God, then at least in the treatment. They didn't have to have a lot of faith to see results either. Just a little could make a world of difference—even a grain of faith the size of a mustard seed.

It became clear to me that the greatest danger my stepfather's patients faced was not physical blindness but spiritual blindness. As the physical darkness closed in, the spiritual darkness loomed as well—a "darkness that one can feel" (Ex 10:21). So the patients were effectively waging their war against blindness on two fronts. One of them—the physical—was not always winnable. The other, more important front could be won, but the soldiers were often demoralized, unaware of the powerful arms at their disposal.

I know what it is like to lose my spiritual vision. I also know what it is like to regain it. The experiences are as different as night and day.

◆ ◆ ◆

I wrote the following in September 2005 while working on the first edition of this book at the Morning Star House of Prayer, a retreat house near the Delaware River, on the outskirts of Trenton, New Jersey (which is beautiful, contrary to what you may have heard about the Garden State):

> The house where I am staying is run by a pair
> of nuns who have retired from teaching. One of
> them, Sister Gerry, has been blind since the age
> of twenty-four due to a genetic disorder. Now
> eighty-two, she is remarkably vibrant, despite
> having cancer.
>
> Have you ever met someone who positively
> *radiated* grace? I have had that experience on rare
> occasions, nearly always in the presence of some-
> one old and frail. It seems that God gives some-
> thing extra to older people who are suffering
> pain or a disability—if they're open to receiving
> it.
>
> Sister Gerry has that inner glow of one who
> has asked the Lord with all her heart to make her

an instrument of his love and peace. Her eyes sparkle in a way that I've never witnessed in a blind person.

The other day, I discussed with Sister Gerry a book she had cowritten about the founder of her religious order, *Forever Yes: The Story of Lucy Filippini*. A copy of the book was in my room at the retreat, and I'd begun reading about how the shy young woman living in seventeenth-century Italy reacted when the church asked her to direct schools for girls and women.

Lucy went through an intense, dark period of soul-searching, feeling uncertain of God's will. Finally, feeling no comfort or consolation despite her prayers, she stepped out in faith—"quivering" out a "yes," as the book puts it.

Once Lucy made the decision to accept the daunting task, her comfort and consolation returned. But she had to take that first step on her own.

The story reminded me so much of my own life—times when, feeling trapped in darkness, I had taken a halting step out into the light. I might have felt stuck in an unsatisfying job or relationship, or just in a rut.

My experience of darkness could include fear of disappointment, fear of failing publicly, fear of ridicule, or all of the above. Most of all, I feared that there might be *nothing* out there for me—no job, boyfriend, or life worth living outside the familiar unhappiness that had become unbearable. When you are facing that kind of hopelessness, you need more than ordinary strength to open the door that leads to a life of hope and opportunity.

A Protestant pastor, David Ireland, has a good analogy to describe what it's like to put one's faith in action.[1] He says it's like being a child on the third floor of a burning building, looking down and seeing a strong man with open arms. The man is saying, "Jump!"

You look at the man and you know that he is capable of catching you. You look back and you see the fire getting closer. Yet simply knowing that the man is capable of catching you doesn't make it easy to jump.

The fire keeps getting closer, and the man keeps calling, "Jump! I'll catch you!"

Finally, when you're certain that staying in the building one moment longer will kill you, you let go of your uncertainty and terror—and jump.

During the times in my life when I had to jump, God was always there to catch me. But, like the child in Ireland's story—and like Lucy Filippini—I endured a terrifying moment as I leaped into the air, before I could land safely in his everlasting arms.

I told Sister Gerry of the memories that her description of Lucy's anguish—and the eventual comfort she received—brought back to me. Then she told me that she had drawn upon personal experience as she and her coauthor, a fellow nun, wrote that part of the book.

It was her reaction to becoming blind.

"I realized I had a choice," she said. Either she could believe her life was over or she could say yes to blindness and trust in what God had in store for her.

Looking at Sister Gerry—seeing her deep brown eyes with their improbable sparkle—I couldn't doubt that she had made the right choice. She had given so much to the world—and still had so much to give. Her existence alone was a gift.

Seventeen months after I wrote those words, Sister Gerry passed away.

On the website of the Morning Star House of Prayer is a poem Sister Gerry wrote to those close to her, a kind of spiritual last will and testament.[2] She begins: "I say, thank you, because in hundreds of different ways, you have been for me a light."

After listing several ways that those close to her brought light to her life, Sister Gerry writes, "Now that I have made the transition from this life to a new life, I promise to hold each of you in my heart and to be your advocate before the throne of God." Then she closes the poem with these words:

> My prayer for you is, "Let your light shine before
> all that they may see the good that you do and
> give glory to God, the Source of all light."
> I will always love you.
>
> Sister Geraldine Calabrese

The promise Sister Gerry makes to hold those close to her in her heart, to intercede for them, and to always love them, reminds me of a thought that came to me a few years ago when the pain of loneliness was hitting me particularly hard. I had feelings for a man who was unavailable. (At the time, I was studying theology at a Catholic seminary, where practically *every* man is unavailable.)

The man was kind to me, in the manner of chaste friendship, and his kindness awakened in me the longing for someone to fill the hole in my heart that cannot be filled. It is a very old longing, predating even the time when I first began to feel sexual attraction. (I mean, I can remember being four years old and wanting to be special to Mickey Mouse.)

Somewhere mixed in with this longing was, I thought, genuine love for the man who sparked it. But when I reflected upon my feelings, I could not honestly tell to what degree they comprised love for this man in his individuality and to what degree they comprised love for what he represented in my imagination.

During that time, I was reading the first letter of St. John, in which, as Augustine has noted, nearly everything is about charity—the *agape* love that unites us to God and to one another.[3] Something in that letter—and I wish I could remember what it was—brought to mind St. Paul's words in his great hymn to charity: "Love never ends" (1 Cor 13:8 RSV). I realized at that moment, for the first time, that if there was anything true about my feelings for that man— any love for the person he really was and not for a fantasy I had built based on a wish of what he could be to me—then I would be able to show him that love in heaven. Likewise, whatever genuine love he had for me would be revealed to me in heaven, purified of lust, woundedness, self-love, and all the other things that prevent people from fully embodying God's love to one another in this life.

The thought brought to mind St. Paul's teaching that, on the last day, everyone's works will be "revealed with fire": if a person's work, having been tried by fire, is shown to truly stand upon Christ as its foundation, that person will receive a reward (see 1 Cor 3:10–15). Whatever is genuine in my love for any human being is not wasted. It will have to withstand purification by the fiery love of Jesus' own Sacred Heart. But if it survives such purification, not only will it remain in heaven, but also it will actually contribute to my meriting heaven.

Contemplating these scriptural teachings consoled me, because they gave meaning to my suffering. It *is* a kind of suffering when one feels love that cannot be fulfilled in this life, and it is a consolation to know that this love, however discomfiting it feels at the moment, will one day be purified into a thing of everlasting beauty. That beauty is present even now in the love of those whose selfless outreach brings Christ to others—as Sister Gerry did when, in the final stages of cancer, she wrote to all those whose lives had touched hers, "I will always love you."

◆ ◆ ◆

Our culture misunderstands the nature of disappointment. Advertisers try to convince us to buy brand-name products rather than risk disappointment by taking a chance on unknown brands. Pornography purveyors seek to persuade men and women to take their sexual pleasure right now from a distorted image of an anonymous body rather than risk rejection in the future by a real, live, flesh-and-blood human being. Always, we are warned that this may be our last chance. Like the advertising tagline that warns, "This offer will expire in thirty days," we're told that our odds of being married will expire after we hit age thirty.

What do we do when this fear gains a foothold? We go spiritually blind and grasp at the air, like the frantic game-show contestants in a glass booth who have thirty seconds to snatch as many one-hundred-dollar bills as they can. We latch on to the first nonrepulsive love interest who breezes our way and end up facing just what we were trying so hard to avoid: disappointment.

It is the fear of disappointment that disappoints. The happiest, most fulfilled people are those who have overcome this fear. Only then are they free to display all the graces that have been given them. They have hope, and as Paul wrote, "hope does not disappoint" (Rom 5:5).

One evening as I was finishing the original edition of this book, I had dinner at a midtown Manhattan restaurant with Harry Mount, a visiting English newspaper journalist who had a kind of clinical curiosity about my conversion. He peppered me with questions about chastity, even suggesting that maybe, given that I'd been looking for so long, I might not find the man I was looking for.

His tone put me on the defensive. "That's not true," I responded. "My chances are better now than they've ever been, because before I was chaste, I was looking for love in all the wrong places. It's only now that I'm truly ready for marriage and have a clear vision of the kind of man I want for my husband. "I may be thirty-seven," I concluded, "but in husband-seeking years, I'm only twenty-two."

Today, I look back at that answer and, even having since discerned a call to consecrated celibacy, I think I said the right thing. I *was* gaining a clear vision of the kind of love I wanted. It just wasn't yet clear enough.

◆ ◆ ◆

Some people spend long hours praying for a sign to show them what they're meant to do with their lives. A particular word might come to them in prayer—a friend of mine once got the word "Philadelphia"—and then they'll spend more hours praying to discern what *that* means.

Personally, although I do pray for guidance at times when unsure of which direction to take, I don't believe it normally takes any great effort to discern God's will. Once we begin to realize our complete dependence on the Lord for all things, striving to recognize and share the love he gives us, he gives us a sure sign that our will is aligned with his.

The sign is gratitude—our own gratitude. If you are unhappy, showing gratitude to God can ultimately help you find a way out of your troubles, as I discovered years ago when, during a particularly bad economic recession, I was out of work for many months. I prayed every day for a job, but when none of my efforts to find one panned out, it was hard to keep my hopes up.

One day, saying my morning prayers as I walked to the train station so I could "pound the pavement" in New York City, a different prayer than usual came to mind:

"Thank you, God, for all the things you have done in my life, thank you for all the things you are doing in my life, and thank you for all the things you *will do* in my life." There was something about the feeling of thanking God in advance that changed my perspective. I didn't feel like a victim anymore. No matter what happened, I felt secure that the Lord had everything in hand. More than that, I believed he would enable me to be an active participant in his plan.

When I first prayed that prayer, I was Protestant. Today, I can pray it as a Catholic, and I do, as part of my thanksgiving after receiving Holy Communion. It reminds me that I am not alone. Jesus was with me throughout my past, loving me even before I knew him; he is with me now in a new way through my Baptism, and so long as I do not seek to remove myself from his presence, he will remain with me at every point of my journey.

◆ ◆ ◆

There is a scene in C. S. Lewis's Chronicles of Narnia novel *The Magician's Nephew* in which Aslan, the lion who represents Christ, sings Narnia and all the universe around it into existence. His voice seems to thunder from every direction, shaking the very air. Perhaps that is an apt allegory for the creation of the universe. Yet the universe is also re-created at every moment, in that its continued existence depends upon God's continuing to sustain it.

What impresses me is that the voice that holds all things in existence is not the voice of thunder that Lewis imagines. It is, rather, a still, small voice like the voice that spoke to Elijah in the cave (1 Kgs 19:12). It is the voice I heard at Mass today, when Jesus, through a priest, spoke the words that brought his body back to earth from heaven; it is the voice I hear in the words of consecration at every Mass.

A Protestant denomination some years ago had a slogan designed to highlight its "creative" approach to worship: "God is still speaking." In a manner in which that denomination would not dare to acknowledge, that statement is literally true. God is still speaking the world into existence; he is still speaking his own very body, blood, soul, and divinity onto every Catholic Church's altar. He is doing it in the words of consecration, the words that he spoke nearly two thousand years ago in a voice that transcends time; these words have formed an unbroken chain passed from generation to generation by the laying on of hands.

Have you seen how the entire world all but disappears for a split second at the consecration of the Host at Mass? It happens very quickly, and if you blink you will miss it. Everything in the created universe is revealed to be hanging as though suspended, as though the fabric of reality were as fragile as a bubble dangling from a leaf. The only thing that is fully real, fully true, and fully grounded is the elevated Host and the words pouring from the priest's lips that telescope time and space to the Last Supper.

Benedict XVI, in his Christmas 2006 homily, spoke of how the Church Fathers found in the Greek Old Testament a phrase expressing how, in the Incarnation, "God made himself small so that we could understand him, welcome him, and love him."[4] The words they found were in Isaiah 10:23, which in the Greek translation says, "God made his Word short, he abbreviated it."[5]

I thought about how God's voice, making itself small to meet our smallness, sustains our fragile existence while praying this past Sunday at the Georgetown Jesuit Cemetery, where I often go to remember the souls there as well as all my family and friends who have passed on. Entering the cemetery that day, I encountered a large, stunning spider web hanging from a weeping evergreen. It was the most beautiful web I have ever seen in my life. The web was visible only because I was approaching it from the west, and so the midafternoon sun was shining brightly on it from that direction. When I passed by it and looked back, it was all but invisible except for a very slight sparkle in the air.

As I paused to pray at the grave of Brother Francis C. Schroen, S.J., the lay brother who created the gorgeous paintings that decorate Georgetown's Gaston Hall, an Eastern Tiger Swallowtail butterfly flew in from the west, fluttering directly over the headstone in front of me. I turned to see it continue flying east, going over the cemetery and then curving sharply upward. It went toward the top of the adjacent building (about fifty feet up) before it disappeared from sight.

Later that day, I had a tour of a Melkite Catholic church, and the subdeacon leading the tour talked about how the icons on the ceiling ran from west to east. The East represents Eden and, by extension, heaven, he explained, while the west represented distance from God, that is, judgment and condemnation. The images on the western side of the church's ceiling included John the Baptist and other saints pointing toward the eastern side—prophets seeking to turn the viewer away from condemnation and toward the vision of God. Hearing this confirmed for me the beautiful symbolism that I had intuited of the butterfly, as a traditional symbol of resurrection, flying from the west over Brother Schroen's grave and up toward the east and heaven. I thought too about how the spider web was visible when I was walking east but not when I was walking west. It is as if to say that only if I follow that butterfly flying east toward heaven, keeping my eyes on God, will I recognize snares. I will fail to see them if I walk in the opposite direction.

20

CRAVING HEAVEN

When one friend of mine heard the title of this book, she assumed it was going to be about drawing energy and excitement from repressed sexual desires—what Sigmund Freud called "sublimation."

In fact, I don't believe resisting sexual temptation necessarily leaves one with oodles of pent-up urges just waiting to be redirected. If that were true, then by now, I would have accomplished something big, *really* big. I mean, I would have either found a cure for cancer or, failing that, crafted the largest rubber-band ball known to mankind.

The thrill of the chaste is something else entirely.

♦ ♦ ♦

The Freudian belief that sexual frustration may be turned toward higher goals assumes there is something in the nature of such frustration that is essentially good.

Now, there is good to be found in sexual *desire*. The capacity for it is an essential part of our makeup. Likewise, there is good contained in the desire for eating and drinking. Sex, however, is different from eating and drinking in that it is not necessary for individual survival. Because of this, we are able to control our desire for sex to a far greater extent than we can control our desire for food and drink.

Sexual frustration—as opposed to simple desire—means being preoccupied with the unfulfilled desire for sex to the point where it takes precedence over other desires or otherwise interferes with one's mental health. The equivalent in terms of eating or drinking would be an addiction that causes one to obsess over a substance that would not be harmful in moderation but, again, is not really needed to live. For example, it's natural to desire something to drink but not to crave a particular mind-altering drink so much that it impairs one's ability to function.

When you encounter a friend with an alcohol problem who is making a sincere go at kicking the habit, you don't say to him or her, "Just think of all the things you can do with your alcoholic frustration now that you're able to put it to good use." The frustration that accompanies the alcoholic's craving may be a powerful force, but it is a negative one. It can't create. It can only destroy.

But what of the craving itself? Granting that there is good contained in the desire for things necessary for life or for propagating new life, can there be something good in craving even when it is for something harmful, as with the alcoholic? And, if so, when the one who suffers this craving resists pursuing the harmful object of his or her desire, can any part of this goodness be salvaged? You may be surprised to learn that the answer given by the Catholic Church is a resounding yes.

◆ ◆ ◆

St. Augustine, as with many of the Church Fathers, saw that there was confusion among the faithful over how to interpret St. Paul's exhortation, "Pray without ceasing" (1 Thes 5:17). It was fine for a hermit to spend every waking moment uttering prayers, but what about the rest of us, saddled with work and family responsibilities?

The answer Augustine offered is in his beautiful Letter 130, written to Proba, a widow who requested his advice on how to pray. He tells Proba that to pray without ceasing is to desire the gift of God himself without ceasing.[1] In another work, commenting on Psalm 38:9, "Lord, all my longing is known to thee" (RSV), he says that your very desire for God is your prayer, and "if your desire is continuous, your prayer is continuous."[2]

Such desire is a thirst for God that is made possible by God's own thirst for souls, as the *Catechism of the Catholic Church* explains in a beautiful paraphrase of Augustine's teaching, citing Jesus' words to the Samaritan woman: "'If you knew the gift of God! [Jn 4:10].' The wonder of prayer is revealed beside the well where we come seeking water: there, Christ comes to meet every human being. It is he who first seeks us and asks us for a drink. Jesus thirsts; his asking arises from the depths of God's desire for us. Whether we realize it or not, prayer is the encounter of God's thirst with ours. God thirsts that we may thirst for him" (CCC 2560).

Even when, seeing God with the eyes of the heart, we do in some sense recognize the encounter of his thirst with ours, we are not to therefore cease seeking him. Rather, we are to exercise our desire for him by thirsting for him all the more. This continuous desire purifies the believer's heart, enlarging it to create more room for God to dwell within. It is for this reason that, knowing that our thirst for God is not to be fully satisfied in this life, we desire him with what Augustine calls a "learned ignorance."[3] Augustine takes his inspiration for the expression from the words of St. Paul: "Likewise the Spirit helps us in our weakness; for we do not know how to pray as we ought, but the Spirit himself intercedes for us with sighs too deep for words" (Rom 8:26 RSV). "Why . . . do we suppose that [Paul] said what he could have said neither thoughtlessly nor mistakenly, unless it is that temporal trouble and tribulations very often are beneficial either for healing the swelling of pride or for testing and practicing patience, for which a more splendid reward is reserved when it is tested and practiced, or for chastising and destroying sins of any sort? But we, who do not know what benefit they bring, long to be delivered from all tribulation."[4]

The word for "swelling" in "healing the swelling of pride" is, in Augustine's Latin, *tumorem*. It can mean simply "swelling," but given the Mystical Body theology that suffuses Augustine's writings, the English derivative "tumor" is also appropriate: pride is here likened to a cancer on the Body of Christ. In building up our desire for God in prayer, we forestall being sated with greed or with anything else that is not God, and so heal the tumors that threaten to close up our hearts.

◆ ◆ ◆

The idea that human desire is not to be fully satisfied in this life was no more fashionable in Augustine's time than it is today. Yet it was then, and is now, a deeply healing truth, one that changes lives.

On a rainy night in 1940, Alcoholics Anonymous founder Bill W. was experiencing an emotional and spiritual crisis, as his efforts to spread the word about his recovery group were bearing little fruit. A visitor came to his door; he reluctantly opened it to find a stranger: Father Edward Dowling, S.J., a nonalcoholic who sought him out after being struck by the similarity between AA's Twelve Steps and St. Ignatius Loyola's rules for spiritual discernment.

Soon Bill was talking about all the steps and
taking his fifth step (telling the exact nature of
his wrongs) with this priest who had limped in
from a storm. He told Father Ed about his anger,
his impatience, his mounting dissatisfactions.
"Blessed are they," Father Ed said, "who hunger
and thirst."

When Bill asked whether there was ever to
be any satisfaction, the priest snapped, "Never.
Never any." Bill would have to keep on reaching.
In time, his reaching would find God's goals, hidden in his own heart.[5]

By worldly standards, Father Ed's answer should have
been dispiriting; yet, for Bill W., it brought great comfort
and peace.[6] Desire cannot truly be frustrated if the act of
desiring itself puts one in contact with God. In G. K. Chesterton's words, "The riddles of God are more satisfying
than the solutions of man."[7]

◆ ◆ ◆

St. Thomas Aquinas asks in his *Summa Theologiae*, "Is sorrow to be shunned more than pleasure is to be sought?"[8] If
you replace "sorrow" with "loneliness," I think the answer
modern culture gives is an unqualified yes. Loneliness is
seen as equal to unhappiness, and it is to be avoided at all
costs. Fleeing it is perhaps the easiest of temptations. It is
especially easy because, in many of its manifestations—
such as avoiding introspection, burying oneself in work,
or networking electronically with friends—it does not feel
like a vice.

But the Angelic Doctor thinks differently. We are
designed in such a way, Aquinas says, that we are able to
pursue pleasure more eagerly than we avoid pain, and since
grace builds on nature, there is an "ought" behind that "is."

The pleasure we are to pursue, he makes clear, is not mere hedonism. Pleasure for Aquinas "is desirable for the sake of the good which is its object." The highest pleasure, then, is the delight whose object is the supreme good, beatitude, which is the perfect union of the soul with God.

We enter into that beatitude through living out the Beatitudes, and the very first of them requires that we allow, within our innermost being, an empty space. "Blessed are the poor in spirit, for theirs is the kingdom of heaven" (Mt 5:3). Only when we stop trying to lose ourselves in temporal and perishable external riches can we begin to realize that we already possess treasures in clay.

The amount of space we make in our hearts for God determines not only whether we receive beatitude but also how much of it we receive, as St. Thérèse of Lisieux shows in her *Story of a Soul*. Thérèse, who looked to Augustine as a master of prayer,[9] was acutely conscious of her need to turn what she called the "immensity" of her desires toward her divine Spouse, who alone could fulfill them. Writing to her sister Pauline, Thérèse recalls how, as a child, she was "astonished . . . that God does not give equal glory in heaven to all His chosen":

> I was afraid they were not all equally happy. You made me bring Daddy's big tumbler and put it by the side of my tiny thimble. You filled them both with water and asked me which was the fuller. I told you they were both full to the brim and that it was impossible to put more water in them than they could hold. And so . . . you made me understand that in heaven God will give His chosen their fitting glory and that the last will have no reason to envy the first.[10]

The reader of Thérèse's autobiography knows that, despite the Little Flower's relief at the assurance that there would be no reason for envy in heaven, she herself had no intention of being a "thimble." On the contrary, longing to be filled with God, she stretched out her hand and declared "I choose all"—everything the Lord willed for her, including suffering.[11]

In her holy desire to pour herself out in a sacrifice of love, Thérèse, like Augustine, finds her model in Christ, who stretched out his arms on the Cross to show the faithful how they are to stretch out toward God and neighbor. Augustine says that when the faithful, grounded in grace, hearts lifted up in "expectation of the things that are above," live out their baptismal union with Christ crucified, their imitation of Jesus puts them into contact with his love. Those who have sought his face will receive his own fullness into the awaiting vacuum within their purified hearts: "[Extend] yourself now, if you can, to the recognition of Christ's love, a recognition that surpasses all other knowledge. When you have reached that point, you will be filled with all the fullness of God. Then will be experienced that *face to face* [1 Cor 13:12]. You will be filled, of course, with the fullness of God, not so that God is full of you but so that you are full of God."[12]

When I contemplate these words of the Doctor of Grace in light of that hole in my heart that cannot be filled, I realize that loneliness, while not good in itself, can be turned to the greatest good. It can set us on the path to the highest heaven, provided we are willing to follow it as far as it goes—to the Cross.

◆ ◆ ◆

I completed the original edition of this book in December 2005, during the weeks leading up to Christmas—my last Christmas as a Protestant, for I was preparing to be received into the Church. It ends with a reflection that reveals where I was in my journey at the time:

When I was in second grade, I had a teacher who insisted that students give out valentines to everyone in the class—not just their friends—on Valentine's Day. It was an ill-considered move to keep unpopular students from feeling left out.

As one who's always been in with the out crowd, I should have benefited from the teacher's valentine system. But I didn't. The valentines I received didn't make me feel special, because I knew that whoever gave them to me was also giving them to everyone else. There was no element of surprise, no sense that my cards were gifts intended just for me.

I would rather receive one real valentine from someone giving it to me from the heart than receive a million from people sending them out of a sense of obligation.

Before I was chaste, when I was giving off signals that I was sexually available, interest from men didn't mean to me what it means now. I was still happy when a man I found attractive found me attractive, but there was a definite sense of causation: I'm wearing a low-cut blouse, I'm saying hello to this man before he says hello to me, I'm smiling seductively and making eye contact with him, touching his shoulder, touching his arm, fluttering my eyelashes, and so on. With all those "I'm available" cues, of course he'll flirt back if he's available and finds me the least bit attractive.

Now when I receive interest from a man who interests me, it's far more exciting. I'm no longer carrying a neon sign that reads "Easy," nor am I playing hard to get. I'm dressing in a way that plays up my beauty while retaining a sense of mystery. Most of all, I'm being who I am, striving to display all the spiritual graces that have been given me. If a desirable man sees all these things and is drawn to me because of them,

then there's a real chance that what attracts him
most is something inside me—something that
will still be there when my wrinkles multiply.
    That kind of attraction is the one special val-
entine. You only need to receive it once in your
life—and it's yours forever.

Reading that conclusion now, I am thankful that those
words, and *The Thrill of the Chaste* as a whole, have helped
many readers counter the culture as they seek lasting love.
I am thankful too that many readers have found such love,
including a married book editor who, having been encouraged by *The Thrill* during her single years, sought to repub-
lish it for a Catholic audience (hence the edition you now
hold in your hands).

But am I thankful for where I am today—having consecrated my celibacy rather than continuing to seek a husband who might be that "one special valentine"? The short
answer is yes. The long answer is that, when I chose to consecrate my celibacy, I did not do so because I was giving up
on the hope of marriage. I made the consecration because I
realized that marriage would not satisfy me. In retrospect,
I can see the beginnings of that realization in a reflection I
posted five years ago on my blog:

> Much of the pain of loneliness felt by the unmar-
> ried—whether that of not being in a relation-
> ship, or that of being in a one-sided affair of the
> heart—comes, I think, from forgetting what it
> means to be as little children.
>   Jesus told his disciples, "Unless you turn
> and become like children, you will not enter the
> kingdom of heaven" (Mt 18:3). I think about that
> a lot, because children truly do experience a taste
> of heaven in a manner that can seem barred to
> single adults whose desires have "matured."
> They experience the most fulfilling happiness in
> the love of family and friends—without feeling

the lack of spousal love that enters into adults in hope of marriage.

It is so easy to make a curious baby smile. When his eyes meet yours, all you have to do is break into an expression of joy, and the child's lips and eyes spontaneously melt into a look of delight. Poignantly, the same is true if you frown; his face will likewise fall, and he may even cry.

True, one could say that the baby's change of expression is not true empathy, because he does not yet fully understand you as an "other" outside himself. But even if he is not willfully feeling what you feel, there is something Godlike in the child's natural reaction that is all too often lost in the considered response of the grown-up. For God's response to our joy or sorrow is *not* a considered one. It is immediate. He rejoices with those who rejoice and weeps with those who weep (Rom 12:15). Just thinking about our need for his redemptive sacrifice caused Jesus to sweat drops of blood, each one of which was enough to redeem the whole world. His goodness cannot help but diffuse itself. The baby's reflexive smile is an image of the smile of God.

The liturgy of the Mass forces us to "turn and become like children" when we say the Our Father before receiving Communion. We are reminded of our need for God to smile upon us— and are immediately rewarded as he bestows his peace upon us. That gift is, in turn, swiftly surpassed by the gift of peace in the world to come as well, through the Eucharist that brings heaven to earth.

For an unmarried adult, perhaps the most sorrowful words in the English language are the frighteningly popular expressions "only a friend" or "just friends." Only when we are adults do we add such qualifiers. As children, there is no greater joy than simply having a friend at all.

Although I have not heard the call to the consecrated life, I often think that priests and religious must be the happiest people on earth— and not just because polls indicate they are. Having chosen not to seek fulfillment in an earthly spouse, they are, paradoxically, able to experience shared joy and undiluted happiness with those close to them—much as children do with their playmates. Their relationships are based on a here-and-now appreciation of their friends, opening up the possibility of experiencing a kind of "untimed time" with them. It is fellowship lived in the present tense, freed from the limiting condition that the relationship progress into something more "meaningful."[13]

Looking back, I realize that, even as I wrote those words, God was leading me to a vocation where I could better experience that "untimed time." It is a new kind of "thrill of the chaste." The world is no longer my meat market—it stopped being that for me years ago—and it is no longer my waiting room. It is my cathedral, and every human being is a tabernacle of Christ.

NOTES

2. Why It's Easy to Blame Mom and Dad (and Why You Shouldn't)

1. It is important to note that my memories are my own. My mother does not remember the abuse I suffered during my childhood, or her reaction to it, as I do. What she does remember, she regrets deeply.

2. For the importance of what we do with God's gift of sexuality, see chapter 5.

3. If you have a parent who is actively abusive, know that forgiveness does not require making yourself vulnerable to someone who is likely to harm you. Forgiveness in Catholic teaching refers to the interior act of asking God to forgive the offender (see *Catechism of the Catholic Church* 2842, 2843). In no way does it depend upon the other person's willingness to reconcile, neither does it mean forgoing the demands of justice or pretending that an evil act was not evil. For more on forgiveness, see chapter 5 of my book *My Peace I Give You: Healing Sexual Wounds with the Help of the Saints* (Notre Dame, IN: Ave Maria Press, 2012).

3. My Journey Home (to Rome)

1. See John W. Lynch, *Bernadette: The Only Witness* (Boston: St. Paul Editions, 1981), 26.

2. Patricia A. McEachern, *A Holy Life: St. Bernadette of Lourdes* (San Francisco: Ignatius Press, 2005), 68.

3. See Martin Gardner, *The Annotated Alice* (New York: W.W. Norton, 2000), 144–145.

4. Second Vatican Council, *Gaudium et Spes* § 22.

5. For more on the Catholic tradition of making a daily offering, see the beautiful book by James Kubicki, S.J., *A Heart on Fire: Rediscovering Devotion to the Sacred Heart of Jesus* (Notre Dame, IN: Ave Maria Press, 2012).

6. For more reflections on redemptive suffering, including stories from the lives of saints who found healing from the wounds of trauma and abuse, see *My Peace I Give You*.

4. The First Cut Is the Deepest

1. G. K. Chesterton, *The Autobiography of G. K. Chesterton* (San Francisco: Ignatius Press, 2006), 324 (originally published in 1936).

2. "For I know the plans I have for you, says the Lord, plans for welfare and not for evil, to give you a future and a hope" (Jer 29:11, RSV).

3. Sheen discusses the psychological benefits of sacramental confession in his book *Peace of Soul* (New York: McGraw-Hill, 1949; repr., Liguori, MO: Triumph Press, 1996).

4. See chapter 10 for more on this.

5. The Meaning of Sex

1. Brian Alexander, "Free Love: Was There a Price to Pay?" *MSNBC*, June 22, 2007, http://www.nbc-news.com/id/19053382/ns/health-sexual_health/t/free-love-was-there-price-pay/#.U-zrG6PiJw0.

2. Eric Sammons, "Father Cutié and the Pelvic Trinity" (blog), June 2, 2010, http://ericsammons.com/blog/2010/06/02/fr-Cutié-and-the-pelvic-trinity (original page is offline, but accessible through the Internet Archive Wayback Machine, http://archive.org).

3. Fulton J. Sheen, *Treasures in Clay* (New York: Doubleday, 2008), 309.

4. Sammons, "Father Cutié."

5. Ibid.

6. Pope Paul VI, *Humanae Vitae* § 7.

7. Ibid.

8. Ibid.

9. John Paul II, *Male and Female He Created Them*, 220 (TOB 25:3, General Audience of April 2, 1980). When making this statement, the pope added that his words referred to *Humanae Vitae* § 7.

10. John Paul II, General Audience, November 28, 1984, http://www.ewtn.com/library/PAPALDOC/jp2tb128.htm.

11. Second Vatican Council, *Gaudium et Spes* § 24.

12. Quoted in Pope Benedict XVI, General Audience, August 13, 2008, http://www.vatican.va/holy_father/benedict_xvi/audiences/2008/documents/hf_ben-xvi_aud_20080813_en.html.

13. On this point, see Pope Paul VI, *Humanae Vitae* § 9.

6. Gaining Self-Control without Losing Your Mind

1. See John Zmirak, *The Bad Catholic's Guide to Good Living* (New York: Crossroad, 2005), 28.

2. On what the Church means when it speaks of "free, faithful, total, and fruitful" married love, see Pope Paul VI, *Humanae Vitae* § 9.

3. John Paul II, General Audience, January 12, 1983.

4. St. Ambrose, *Hexameron* VI, ix, 68, trans. John J. Savage, quoted in Nicolas James Perella, *The Kiss: Sacred and Profane* (Berkeley: University of California Press, 1969), 29.

5. St. Ambrose, *Epistola* 41, quoted in Perella, *The Kiss*, 28.

6. Perella, *The Kiss*, 28. The reference is to Augustine's Sermon 229.

7. Pope Francis, *Lumen Fidei* § 27.

8. Ibid., § 32.

9. CCC 1704, quoting Second Vatican Council, *Gaudium et Spes* § 15.

10. G. K. Chesterton, *The Everlasting Man*, in *Collected Works of G. K. Chesterton*, vol. 2 (San Francisco: Ignatius Press, 1986), 388.

11. G. K. Chesterton, *George Bernard Shaw* (New York: John Lane, 1909), 6.

12. G. K. Chesterton, *Orthodoxy* (New York: John Lane, 1909), 223. Pope Benedict XVI referred to the Chesterton quotation during an interview for German television on August 5, 2006 "(Pope Benedict XVI: 'We Have a Positive Idea to Offer,'" accessed May 1, 2014, http://www.dw.de.)

13. Eden, *My Peace I Give You*, 37–38.

7. Becoming a Singular Sensation

1. G. K. Chesterton, *Tremendous Trifles* (New York: Dodd, Mead, 1920), 7.

2. St. Augustine, *Confessions* I.1, in *Nicene and Post-Nicene Fathers*, ed. Philip Schaff, First Series, vol. 1 (Buffalo, NY: Christian Literature Publishing, 1887), revised and edited by Kevin Knight, New Advent, accessed May 1, 2014, http://www.newadvent.org/fathers/110101.htm.

3. Second Vatican Council, *Dei Verbum* § 21.

8. The Agony and the Ecstasy

1. Charles Dickens, *A Christmas Carol* (London: Bradbury & Evans, 1858), 17.

2. Eden, *My Peace I Give You*, 69.

3. Dorothy Day, *The Long Loneliness* (New York: HarperCollins, 1997), 140 (originally published in 1952).

4. Quote from a 2004 episode of *Sex and the City*, IMDb, accessed July 8, 2014, http://www.imdb.com/title/tt0698612/quotes.

9. Saying Yes Like You Mean It

1. On the divine indwelling and Baptism, see *CCC* 260, 1987, 1988.

2. Fulton J. Sheen, *The World's First Love* (New York: McGraw-Hill, 1952), online at http://archive.org/stream/TheWorldsFirstLove/SheenTheWorldsFirstLoveedited.txt. The image of the sword comes from St. Luke's account of the Presentation, when Mary and Joseph brought the infant Jesus to the Temple: "Simeon blessed them and said to Mary his mother, 'Behold, this child is set for the fall and rising of many in Israel, and for a sign that is spoken against

(and a sword will pierce through your own soul also), that thoughts out of many hearts may be revealed'" (Lk 2:34–35 RSV).

3. Pope Pius IX, Apostolic Constitution *Ineffabilis Deus*. See also the *Catechism*'s section on the Immaculate Conception, CCC 490–93.

4. Pope John Paul II, following the tradition of the Church, calls Mary the "Mystical Spouse of the Holy Spirit" in his "Letter to All Consecrated Persons Belonging to Religious Communities and Secular Institutes on the Occasion of the Marian Year" (1988), http://www.vatican. va/holy_father/john_paul_ii/letters/1988/documents/ hf_jp-ii_let_19880522_consecrated-persons_en.html.

5. Second Vatican Council, *Gaudium et Spes* § 24.

6. See CCC 969; Second Vatican Council, *Lumen Gentium* § 62

10. Tender Mercies: Reconnecting with Your Vulnerability

1. Pope Benedict XVI, *Deus Caritas Est* § 1.

2. St. Thomas Aquinas, *Summa Theologiae* II–II, q. 23, a. 1, trans. Fathers of the English Dominican Province (Notre Dame, IN: Christian Classics, 1981).

3. Pope Benedict XVI, *Deus Caritas Est* § 12.

11. The Iniquity of My Heels

1. I recommend seeing a Catholic therapist if a qualified one is available, because secular therapists often see the desire for chastity as evidence of a religious "hangup" that they believe must be overcome. For more information, see my book *My Peace I Give You*, 199–201.

2. Although there are qualified lay spiritual directors, I recommend seeing a priest for spiritual direction if possible. If you cannot find a priest to direct you, you can gain benefits similar to spiritual direction by finding a good confessor and confessing to him regularly (every two weeks or so). For advice on what to look for in a spiritual director and how to find one, see *My Peace I Give You*, 195–99.

3. See Aquinas, *Summa Theologiae* III, q. 8, a. 3.

12. How Beginnings Shape Endings

1. See Erich Fromm, *The Art of Loving* (1956; repr., New York: Continuum, 2008), 4.

2. St. John Chrysostom, *De Compunctionis Cordis* 2.3, quoted by St. Thomas Aquinas in *Summa Theologiae* III, q. 1, a. 4, ad. 3 (Benziger Brothers translation).

3. See Aquinas, *Summa Theologiae* III, q. 65, a. 1.

4. This is a theme found in Lewis's novel *The Great Divorce*. Lewis also hints at this in the final chapter of the last installment of his *Chronicles of Narnia, The Last Battle*.

5. Peter Kreeft, *Fundamentals of the Faith* (San Francisco: Ignatius Press, 1988), 181–87.

13. Answering the Call

1. "Latin Church" refers to what is popularly known in the United States as the Roman Catholic Church, as opposed to Eastern Churches that are in communion with Rome.

2. See Aquinas, *Summa Theologiae* III, q. 65, a. 1.

3. See Second Vatican Council, *Lumen Gentium* § 39.

4. St. Josemaría Escrivá, "Women in Social Life and in the Life of the Church," in *Conversations with Monsignor Escriva de Balaguer*, no. 92 (Dublin: Ecclesia Press, 1972), accessed May 2, 2014, http://www.escrivaworks.org/book/conversations-point-92.htm.

14. The Gift of the Present Moment

1. I have since learned that the hairs were divided among numerous locations where Kolbe is venerated, including the Marytown shrine in Libertyville, Illinois.

15. Living Modestly

1. Kevin Tierney, "Towards a Marian Modesty," *Catholic Exchange*, March 27, 2014, accessed April 10, 2014, http://catholicexchange.com/towards-marian-modesty. Used by permission of the author.

2. Kevin Tierney, "Let's Talk About Modesty," *Catholic Exchange*, January 27, 2014, accessed April 10, 2014, http://catholicexchange.com/lets-talk-modesty. Used by permission of the author.

3. In the Reader's Guide of *My Peace I Give You*, I offer suggestions for choosing a good spiritual director and a good therapist.

4. See Second Vatican Council, *Lumen Gentium* chapter 5, "The Universal Call to Holiness in the Church," and § 39: "In the Church, everyone whether belonging to the hierarchy, or being cared for by it, is called to holiness."

16. A Thorny Issue: Dealing with Temptation

1. Stephen Beale, "Saints and Spiritual Temptation," *Catholic Exchange*, March 20, 2012, accessed April 13, 2014, http://catholicexchange.com/saints-and-sexual-temptation. Used by permission of Catholic Exchange.

2. Pope Francis, Morning Meditation, July 2, 2013, accessed April 13, 2014, http://w2.vatican.va/content/francesco/en/cotidie/2013/documents/papa-francesco-cotidie_20130702_courageous-weakness.html.

3. See Paul S. Loverde, "Bought with a Price Pastoral Letter," accessed April 13, 2014, http://www.arlingtondiocese.org/purity/pastoral_letter.aspx.

4. See St. Augustine, *On Grace and Free Will* 15.

17. Winning the Spiritual Battle

1. Venial sins are those that do not break one of the Ten Commandments, or that are committed without full knowledge and deliberate consent (*CCC* 1857–1858, 1862).

2. Sacramentals are sacred objects and prayers that dispose us to receive the grace that flows from the sacraments (see *CCC* 1667).

3. See Bernard Mulcahy, comp., and Juan-Diego Brunetta, ed., *A Scriptural Rosary for Peace and for the Family*, 2008, accessed April 15, 2014, http://www.kofc.org/un/en/resources/cis/cis319.pdf.

18. Why Shared Values Matter

1. Todd and I remain friends. He is supportive of my apostolate and asked that I refer to him by his real name.

2. See Dwight Longenecker, "Can You Be Good without God?" *Patheos*, April 25, 2012, accessed April 18, 2014, http://www.patheos.com/Catholic/Good-Without-God-Dwight-Longenecker-04-25-2012.

3. St. Augustine, *Confessions* IV.4, in Augustine, *Confessions: Books I–X*, trans. F. J. Sheed (New York: Sheed & Ward, 1942), 54.

4. Robert Ellsberg, "Dearest Forster: The Love Letters of Dorothy Day," *America*, November 15, 2010, accessed April 17, 2014, http://americamagazine.org/issue/755/ideas/dearest-forster.

5. Dorothy Day, *The Long Loneliness*,134.

6. Ibid., 140.

7. Ibid., 236.

8. Ibid., 285.

19. Believing Is Seeing

1. Pastor Ireland used this image in a radio sermon and graciously granted permission for me to relate it in this book.

2. See Geraldine Calabrese, poem, Morning Star Prayer House, accessed April 20, 2014, http://www.morningstarprayerhouse.org/SisterGerry.htm.

3. See Augustine's *Homilies on 1 John*, trans. Boniface Ramsey, prologue (Hyde Park, NY: New City Press, 2008), 19-20.

4. Pope Benedict XVI, "Solemnity of the Nativity of the Lord," December 24, 2006. http://www.vatican.va/holy_father/benedict_xvi/homilies/2006/documents/hf_ben-xvi_hom_20061224_christmas_en.html.

5. Translation from Pope Benedict XVI, "Solemnity of the Nativity of the Lord."

20. Craving Heaven

1. Augustine, Letter 130, 9, 18. All translations of Augustine's Letter 130 are from St. Augustine, *Works*, electronic release of New City Press series, accessed online December 10, 2012, through Intellex Past Masters.

2. Augustine, *Expositions on the Psalms* 37.14. From *Expositions of the Psalms* 33–50, trans. Maria Boulding (Hyde Park, NY: New City Press, 2000), accessed online December 10, 2012, through Intellex Past Masters.

3. Augustine, Letter 130, 15, 28.

4. See Augustine, Letter 130, 14, 25.

5. Robert Fitzgerald, "Father Ed and AA's Bill W.," *Catholic Digest* (April 1991).

6. Ibid.,

7. G. K. Chesterton, "Introduction to the Book of Job," accessed December 11, 2012, http://www.chesterton.org/discover-chesterton/selected-works/the-theologian/introduction-to-job.

8. Aquinas, *Summa Theologiae* I–II, q. 35, a. 6.

9. See St. Thérèse of Lisieux, *The Story of a Soul*, trans. John Clarke, (Washington, DC: ICS Publications, 1976), 258.

10. Ibid., 20–21.

11. Ibid., 27.

12. Augustine, *Expositions on the Psalms* 53.14.15–15.16.

13. Dawn Eden, "Baby Love," *Dawn Patrol* (blog), June 10, 2009, http://dawneden.blogspot.com.

Dawn Eden is a blogger and popular author of *The Thrill of the Chaste: Finding Fulfillment While Keeping Your Clothes On and My Peace I Give You: Healing Sexual Wounds with the Help of the Saints.*

Born into a Jewish family in New York City, Eden lost her faith as a teenager and became an agnostic. During the 1990s, she worked as a rock journalist in New York City, interviewing oldies and classic rock performers. She went on to work for the *New York Post* and the *Daily News*.

At age thirty-one, Eden underwent a dramatic conversion to Christianity that ultimately led her to join the Catholic Church. Both of her books, *The Thrill of the Chaste* (originally published in 2007) and *My Peace I Give You* (2012), have been featured in the *New York Times* and on numerous EWTN programs. Her new version of *The Thrill of the Chaste* is a completely revised and updated Catholic edition of the popular book.

Eden received her pontifical licentiate in sacred theology from the Dominican House of Studies in 2014 and is studying for a doctorate. She has spoken about chastity, spiritual healing, and conversion to thousands of people throughout North America and abroad. She lives in the Chicago area.